TM

WITHDRAWN

RUBEN DARIO IN SEARCH OF INSPIRATION

DOLORES ACKEL FIORE

RUBEN DARIO IN SEARCH OF INSPIRATION

(Greco-Roman mythology in his stories and poetry)

1 9 6 3

LAS AMERICAS PUBLISHING CO.

TO PAUL

with the hope that the curiosity he has shown in
this work throughout most of his six years will
lead someday to an understanding and apprecia-
tion of Rubén and other great poets.

PREFACE

This book is the climax of several years of study and careful thought. My interest in Darío, first awakened in an unusually excellent seminar at Harvard University and sustained throughout my years of graduate study there, culminated in a doctoral dissertation. The intervening years have been devoted both to enlarging and modifying my original work. Specifically, I chose to study Darío's use of Greco-Roman mythology with special reference to the themes of love, beauty and art, as seen in the "cuentos" and his poetry beginning with *Azul* . . . .

It was essential, considering the nature of the subject, to present an analysis of Darío's Latin quotations, the first of its kind, to establish from this point of view just how much he most likely did know of the Latin language and literature. The natural corollary was then to consider his skill in Greek. The problem of his training in the classical languages resolved, I proceeded to discuss his imagery as outlined above. Here, the basic problem was to examine the idea prevalent in Darío criticism that explains this aspect of him in terms of his modern French readings. I have, therefore, offered somewhat of a panorama of these words as they occur in some of the French and Spanish authors Darío knew, to give an indication of how widely diffused they were in both languages. Gathering this documentation was one of the most arduous and frustrating tasks, since the existing dictionaries are of very limited help. Consequently, extensive direct reading had to be done to unearth many of these words.

Since this documentation is vitally important to understand the conclusions drawn, it was deemed advisable to include it, in condensed language, at the beginning of the discussion of each reference. The many parentheses and abbreviations that necessarily resulted seemed more than worthwhile for the sake of the readers' convenience.

I believe I have appropriately acknowledged, in person, the valuable criticisms and help so generously given by many considerate people. Beyond this, I particularly want to express my appreciation to Mr. Gilbert Cam of the New York Public Library, who did everything possible to minimize the inconvenience of pursuing this kind of work in a reference library; to this end, the Frederick Lewis Allen Memorial Room was no small help.

Lastly, I also wish to express my gratitude to my publisher, Mr. Gaetano Massa, whose interest in Spanish literature caused him to undertake the publication of this book as well as those of others before me.

D. A. F.

New York, New York
July, 1962

CONTENTS

CHAPTER I

AN OVER-ALL GLANCE

I *The Need for Renovation*

The last two decades of the nineteenth century marked the coming of a literary revolution that swept through Latin America and later extended to Spain. It was called modernism.[1] In spite of the much-discussed suitability of this name, it has endured in literary history. Modernism embodied many tendencies.[2] It was, above all, a reaction against the excesses of romanticism, not against romanticism *per se*. The influence of the Parnassians and the symbolists combined to declare war on vulgarity of form and expression. Indeed, the initial aim of Rubén Darío and his followers was somewhat negative in

---

[1] In general there were numerous innovating tendencies in the countries of Western Europe during the second half of the nineteenth century, both in literature and in art. Thus we have, among others, the Parnassians, the symbolists, the Pre-Raphaelites and the impressionists. At no time were they grouped under one name. The word *modernism* was used to designate the literary revolt in Latin America. The same word was applied to a tendency within Catholicism that was condemned by Pope Pius X; but this is quite apart from the literary movement that here interests us. See Max Henríquez Ureña, *Breve historia del modernismo*, México, 1954, pp. 9-11. Guillermo Díaz-Plaja in *Modernismo frente a noventa y ocho*, Madrid, 1951, pp. 6-10, sums up the controversy over the incorporation of the word *modernismo* into the *Diccionario de la Real Academia Española*. This word did not make its first appearance in this source until 1899.

[2] Max Henríquez Ureña in *Rodó y Rubén Darío*, La Habana, 1918, pp. 80-87, points out some of the predominant ones. Briefly, a tendency to return to nature, an intense anxiety of spirit, a mysticism that is the artistic enunciation of the eternal mystery, an aristocratic attitude towards the suppression of clichés, the resurrection of ancient Greece and of the gallant festivals of eighteenth-century France. To this he adds, "el conocimiento íntimo y superior de la edad de oro de la literatura española, con un repiqueteo armonioso y lejano de gongorismo, de culteranismo . . ." (I discuss the influence of Góngora on modern literature later in this chapter). A worthwhile presentation of the various ideas on the nature of modernism is to be found in Luis Monguió, "Sobre la caracterización del Modernismo," *Revista Iberoamericana*, VII (noviembre de 1943), 69-80.

11

that they rejected all the existing norms not in harmony with their personal tastes. They were determined to abolish the commonplace words and images that had become so entrenched in the Spanish language.

Certainly, Darío's lexical innovations are best understood in relation to one of the major aspects of Darío criticism, the historical and linguistic, that which has to do with the prevalent style of the period. Actually, Darío was but one of the Spanish-speaking people who felt the need of renovating the language. In the post-Restoration atmosphere, the personality of those who were to form the "Generación del 98" was molded. Simultaneously, South American writers were rebelling against the language of the romantics and the rhetoric of Campoamor and Núñez de Arce. The ideal of the Restoration was order and progress, the reality was a period of carefree living. The taste and ideas of the time submerged Hispanic culture in mediocrity and "ramplonería" that, along with the failure of the last colonial wars, prepared the way for the intellectual movement of the "Generación del 98." Melchor Fernández Almagro has aptly summarized the spirit of the era:

> Una inconsciencia punto menos que infantil regía el ir y venir apasionado de los españoles en relación con las cuestiones que suscitaba la actualidad inmediata. Nadie miraba a lo lejos. Inconsciencia y optimismo. . . . El cuadro de nuestros grandes hombres, para mayor felicidad, estaba cubierto dos veces. De aquí que los españoles se permitiesen el lujo de tener dónde elegir, cifrando su fe en el ídolo público de alguna de las dos series puestas en juego, para satisfacción de toda necesidad banderiza: o Cánovas o Sagasta; o Galdós o Pereda; o Calvo o Vico; o *Lagartijo* o *Frascuelo* . . . Libres de cuidados, las gentes se consagraban a sus ocios predilectos. Triunfaban, con los toreros y los cantantes de ópera, los oradores, los poetas fáciles y los prosistas amenos. Los artículos de fondo sonaban muy bien, y las novelas se multiplicaban con lozanía sin precedente . . .[3]

---

[3] Cited by Pedro Laín Entralgo, *La generación del noventa y ocho,* Buenos Aires, 1947, pp. 46-47. See also José Ortega y Gasset, *Vieja y nueva política,* Madrid, 1914, especially pp. 21-30, where he sharply criticizes Cánovas' view that the Restoration was the "continuación de la historia de España." Ortega y

Prevalent was an oratorical and rhetorical style with long periodic sentences barely separated by a comma or a semicolon. In poetry Spain had the high sounding rhetoric of Núñez de Arce. Most conspicuous because of his oratorical flourishes was Emilio Castelar, who was extremely influential in South America. In fact, Darío pokes fun at him in the story "Un sermón" and in jest coins a word to describe his speech. (See *kalofónico*.) Perhaps the most vitriolic attack on Castelar's platitudes and unpolished sentences was that of González Prada: "Considerándolo bien, es el tambor mayor del siglo XIX: marcha presidiendo el bullicioso batallón de los hombres locuaces, de todos esos inagotables habladores que hablan i hablan por el solo prurito de hablar."[4]

In the midst of the clichés and linguistic triviality, Unamuno stands out as the one who defended with unequaled vigor the need for abandoning the "castellano anquilosado" of the pseudo-classicists:[5]

> Vuelvo a repetirlo: una de las más fecundas tareas que a los escritores en lengua castellana se nos abren es la de forjar un idioma digno de los varios y dilatados países en que se ha de hablar, y capaz de traducir las diversas impresiones e ideas de tan diversas naciones. Y el viejo castellano, acompasado y enfático, lengua de oradores más que de escritores — pues en España los más de estos últimos son oradores por escrito —; . . . el viejo castellano necesita refundición. Necesita para europeizarse a la moderna más ligereza y más precisión a la vez, algo de desarticulación, puesto que hoy tiende a las anquilosis; hacerlo más desgranado, de una sintaxis menos involutiva, de una notación más rápida. La influencia de la lectura de autores franceses va contribuyendo a ello, aun en los que menos se lo creen.[6]

Gasset states: "es que asistimos al fin de la crisis de la Restauración, crisis de sus hombres, de sus partidos, de sus periódicos, de sus procedimientos, de sus ideas, de sus gustos y hasta de su vocabulario; en estos años, en estos meses concluye la Restauración la liquidación de su ajuar; y si se obstina en no morir definitivamente, . . . yo os diría que nuestra bandera tendría que ser ésta: 'La muerte de la Restauración.' 'Hay que matar bien a los muertos'" (p. 22).

[4] Manuel G[onzález] Prada, *Pájinas libres,* Paris, 1894, p. 208.
[5] See Guillermo Díaz-Plaja, *op. cit.,* pp. 156-157.
[6] Miguel de Unamuno, *Ensayos,* Madrid, 1945, I, 318.

Díaz-Plaja believes that the rejection of linguistic cliché by the modernists and the members of the "Generación del 98" was the one point of coincidence between the two groups. However, the motivation of each was quite distinct. The "Generación del 98" sought a functional enrichment of the language "al servicio de la inteligencia . . . rebuscando en la lengua popular regional o en la raíz etimológica."[7] On the other hand, Darío and the rest of the modernists searched for a language filled with beauty and musicality, a language of the select minority.

II *The Role of Spanish Literature*

Considering the dismal state of the Spanish poetic language then, where was Darío to find inspiration for his ambitious task of revitalizing the language? We know that he became particularly fascinated with the Greco-Roman world. Clearly, though, his Greco-Roman vision did not stem so much from a direct reading of the Greek and Latin classics as from his Spanish and modern French readings. Although our main concern is his classical and French background, it seems advisable to discuss briefly Darío's sometimes disputed background in Spanish literature, since he did owe some of his Hellenism to certain poets of the Golden Age as well as to such modern writers as Valera and Menéndez y Pelayo.

An important intellectual stimulus to Darío was his relationship with the Jesuits, which began between 1875 and

[7] Díaz-Plaja, *op. cit.*, p. 190. Compare Unamuno's spirited reply to the accusation that he used words not in the Academy's dictionary: "¡Y las pondrán! Y las pondrán cuando los escritores llevemos a la literatura las voces españolas — españolas, ¿eh? — que andan, y desde siglos, en boca del pueblo." Cited by Rafael Lapesa, *Historia de la lengua española,* 2nd ed., Madrid, 1950, p. 275. Two of the most complete studies on the language problem as viewed by Unamuno have been done by Carlos Blanco Aguinaga, *Unamuno, teórico del lenguaje,* México, 1954, and Fernando Huarte Morton, "El ideario lingüístico de Miguel de Unamuno," *Cuadernos de la Cátedra Miguel de Unamuno,* V (1954), 5-183; in particular, pp. 105-162 discuss Unamuno's ideas on the Spanish language in Spain and South America, the simplification of the orthography, problems of lexicon, "popularismos" and "neologismos."

1878.[8] Darío was presented with such models as Herrera and Lista, and accordingly he began his early poetic work composing odes "al mar, al Sol y a la Virgen María" (EMS, 246). Oddly enough, none of Darío's poems has been found in *El Católico*, the only Jesuit publication of that time. However, Ernesto Mejía Sánchez wisely suggests that perhaps there was a prior Jesuit publication, now unknown, in which some of this youthful poetry appeared. Armando Donoso points out that these same early poetic attempts were also the reflection of lessons learned in Fray Luis, Santa Teresa and Lope.[9] Undoubtedly Darío's most comprehensive study of the Spanish classics was made at the Biblioteca Nacional in Managua (1884) where he read "todas las introducciones de la *Biblioteca de autores españoles* de Rivadeneyra, y las principales obras de casi todos los clásicos de nuestra lengua," according to Darío's own statement in his *Autobiografía*.[10] Donoso indicates that in Darío's *Primeras notas* (1885) there are clear reminiscences of his readings; the Spanish mentors of his adolescence were, according to Donoso, principally Quintana and Núñez de Arce. Darío, in insisting upon his knowledge of the Spanish classics, gives important testimony concerning other influences: "Ha sido deliberadamente que después, con el deseo de rejuvenecer, flexibilizar el idioma, he empleado maneras y construcciones de otras lenguas, giros y vocablos exóticos y no puramente españoles."[11] In the later years, when

---

[8] Ernesto Mejía Sánchez in *Libro jubilar de Alfonso Reyes,* México, 1956, pp. 243-263, has presented a painstaking study of Darío's literary formation prior to his trip to Chile in 1886. This article, "Las humanidades de Rubén Darío," has contributed somewhat to the question of Darío's initiation into the Spanish classics, but, above all, it has brought to light valuable and systematized information on Darío's Greek and Latin education. I discuss this point at some length in the next chapter. All future quotations from this article, to be designated EMS, will be given in the text.

[9] Armando Donoso, "La juventud de Rubén Darío," *Nosotros,* XXXI (1919), 453.

[10] Rubén Darío, *Obras completas,* Madrid, 1917, XV, 33. He adds, "De allí viene que, . . . cosa que sorprendiera a muchos de los que conscientemente me han atacado, el que yo sea en verdad un buen conocedor de letras castizas."

[11] *Autobiografía,* p. 33. It is noteworthy that in this very declaration Darío deliberately uses a non-Spanish construction, the *"que galicado."*

15

Darío was absorbed with Leconte de Lisle, Verlaine, the Goncourts, Flaubert, Moréas, Mallarmé, Laforgue, Régnier and Adam, if he looked to past Spanish writers, it was to Santa Teresa, Góngora and Gracián.[12] With reference to Darío's praise of Góngora in "Trébol" of *Cantos de vida y esperanza* (1905), Marasso points out that Darío was by no means the first one in the nineteenth century to eulogize Góngora. When Darío arrived in France in 1893, he found a sympathy for Gongorism in Verlaine and Moréas, though Verlaine never put Góngora on a plane with Calderón. Góngora was then considered a rebel artist and was already a much-quoted name in reviews and journals. Hugo had earlier touched upon the traditional idea of Góngora in "Encore Dieu:"

Il [Dieu] abuse du gouffre, il abuse du prisme.
Tout, c'est trop. Son soleil va jusqu'au gongorisme;
lumière outrée.[13]

Moreover, in 1891 Laurent Tailhade attempted to establish the similarity of symbolism and Gongorism in his reply to Huret's *Enquête sur l'évolution littéraire*. Marasso correctly maintains that in utilizing in "Trébol" the relationship between Góngora and Velázquez, which Darío probably was already aware of from Adolfo de Castro's comparison made in 1865 and published in the Rivadeneyra collection, Darío was not raising Góngora to the category of "poeta único." In other words, Góngora's name was in the air at that time.

However, Dámaso Alonso, in "Góngora y la literatura contemporánea,"[14] states that the literature of the period had no real contact with Góngora's works. Their admiration for him was superficial and snobbish, so that it does not seem likely that either the symbolists or Darío had a solid knowledge of Góngora. Alonso is rather of the opinion that Darío,

[12] Donoso, *op. cit.,* p. 525.
[13] Quoted by Arturo Marasso, *Rubén Darío y su creación poética,* ed. definitiva, Buenos Aires, 1954, p. 229.
[14] See Dámaso Alonso, *Estudios y ensayos gongorinos,* Madrid, 1955, especially pp. 549-563, where he discusses Góngora and modernism.

while reading the Spanish classics in the Biblioteca Nacional at Managua, must have been astonished by *Polifemo* and the *Soledades*. He does, however, acknowledge having been assured by Antonio Machado that Darío could recite from memory whole stanzas of *Polifemo*. In the light of this testimony, Alonso concedes that Darío may have read *Polifemo*, but not the rest of the typically gongoristic works. Alonso further suggests that at the Biblioteca Nacional Darío may have read the traditionally praised segment of Góngora's works, the "romances" and "letrillas." Therefore, we conclude from this evidence that Darío had no detailed or thorough knowledge of Góngora that would be reflected in Darío's syntax or metaphors. The limited and superficial awareness he did possess could explain, at most, some similarities of vocabulary.

III   *The Role of French Literature*

The study of Darío's background in the French authors of the late nineteenth century will show that a certain amount of his Greco-Roman vocabulary was inspired by the Parnassians and the plastic arts. Tired of the cliché of both the Spanish Golden Age and the modern poetry, Darío found in these Frenchmen "una mina que explotar," a verbal aristocracy that would revitalize the Spanish language, so impoverished, in comparison with French, in the nineteenth century by the tendency to exclude those words that were not *castizo*. However, contrary to opinion, it was not Darío's *Azul* . . . (1888) that introduced those French writers to South America. The years 1880-1890 were, in Argentina, a period of great interest in European readings.[15] Devotion to the French romantics was giving way to the statuesque beauty of the Parnassians. It was the newspapers that revealed the

[15] See María Hortensia Lacau and Mabel Manacorda de Rosetti's excellent article, "Antecedentes del modernismo en la literatura argentina," *Cursos y Conferencias*, XXXI (abril-junio, 1947), 163-92, an invaluable source of information on this problem.

17

Parnassians to the Argentinian intellectual élite. In *La Nación* (1880) there was a study by Ponmartine on the *Poèmes antiques* of Leconte de Lisle, an analysis of the school in its most external aspect: painting and sculpture in verse. In 1883 *El Diario* carried an article by the Parnassian poet Lepelletier, giving the basic facts of the literary history of this school. We see, also, that the columns of these papers were opened to the Parnassians, many of whom did collaborate. Mendès, Silvestre and Coppée did a good deal in *La Nación*. Anatole France, whose articles were published in the most widely read journals of the time, promoted the fame of the Parnassians by his commentaries on Sully Prudhomme, François Coppée and Banville. Sully Prudhomme had no direct collaboration with the Argentinian papers. Mendès assiduously published his stories, especially in *Sud América*. Gautier (1811-1872) and Banville (1823-1891) were the most celebrated, and it is quite possible that Banville's style may have prepared the literary taste for the Darío of *Azul* . . ., for there is a voluptuous air in Banville similar to that of *Azul* . . . . Both Banville and Darío create an atmosphere that transcends refinement and opulence, coupled with a delightful sensuality. The Parnassians, though offering poetic material for a select minority, had immediate repercussions in Argentina. With the publication of Leconte de Lisle's *Apollonide* in 1888, an anonymous article appeared that, in an obvious assimilation of Leconte de Lisle's spirit, is intimately aware of the Hellenic atmosphere.

Darío's really serious and systematized French readings began with his trip to Chile in 1886. While working on *La Época,* which was then reprinting articles of Catulle Mendès and Henri Houssaye, Darío made the acquaintance of two people who were to be of some consequence in his literary formation, Manuel Rodríguez Mendoza and Pedro de Balmaceda. With these two companions, Darío took part in stimulating discussions in the luxurious salons of *La Época,* the Grecian salon filled with marble statues and the eighteenth-century salon with paintings of Watteau and Chardin. The

French influence in Darío came from multiple sources: "Elle s'exerça sur lui, non seulement par les livres qu'il lut en nombre considérable, mais aussi par les décors luxueux des salons où il lisait et travaillait et par les conversations quotidiennes des ses amis et de ses collègues . . . ."[16] In Balmaceda's study, filled with French eighteenth-century art, Darío read copies of *La Nouvelle Revue* and the *Revue Des Deux Mondes,* as well as the Goncourts, Silvestre, Zola, Flaubert, Balzac, Daudet, St. Victor and Mendès. In his *Historia de mis libros,* Darío tells us, "Fué Catulle Mendès mi verdadero iniciador, un Mendès traducido, pues mi francés era precario."[17]

Though admittedly Darío had begun his reading of Hugo and other French authors while in the company of Francisco Gavidia in El Salvador in 1881, these readings were more continuous and systematized during his stay in Chile. Here he acquired a broader taste for the exotic, learned from Th. Gautier, Judith Gautier, Edmond Goncourt and Loti. Beginning with *Azul* . . . it is readily perceived that the Greece and Rome Darío paints is not usually that of mythology itself, but rather that of the gardens of Versailles, interpreted in terms of the elegance and frivolity of eighteenth-century France, very much in the manner of the Goncourt brothers. In "Divagación" (1896) Darío tells us:

> Amo más que la Grecia de los griegos
> la Grecia de la Francia, porque en Francia,
> al eco de las risas y los juegos,
> su más dulce licor Venus escancia.

He does not tell us that France is superior to Greece, but that the French form of the Greek is superior to the ancient,

[16] Erwin K. Mapes, *L'influence française dans l'oeuvre de Rubén Darío,* Paris, 1925, p. 17. The "décors luxueux" were the result of the extravagant taste of Mr. MacClure, wealthy owner of *La Época.*

[17] Cited by Donoso, *op. cit.,* p. 512. However, Mapes, *op. cit.,* pp. 19-20, takes issue with Max Henríquez Ureña and Donoso's conviction that in the era of *Azul* . . . Darío's French was still "precario." Mapes bases his disagreement on the fact that while Darío was at the Biblioteca in Managua, he knew enough French to do some translations of Th. Gautier, which were published in *El Ferrocarril.*

because in France the Greco-Roman culture is more voluptuously refined:

> Demuestran más encantos y perfidias,
> coronadas de flores y desnudas,
> las diosas de Clodión que las de Fidias;
> unas cantan francés, otras son mudas.

The new art initiated in *Azul* . . . culminated in *Prosas profanas* (1896). Darío in the later years cultivated, above all, the symbolists. In fact Darío's studies, published in *La Nación* and later in *Los raros* (1896), were the principal means of these writers becoming known in South America.

IV *Darío Was Not the First To Decry His Environment*

Darío has been bitterly and even unjustly criticized for his preference of distant worlds. He has been labelled "monárquico y anti-republicano,"[18] a servile opportunist, an egoist who, from his ivory tower, looked impassively on mankind's woes. This barrage of less than complimentary remarks stems from an interpretation of Darío's own words in the "Palabras liminares" of *Prosas profanas*: "mas he aquí que veréis en mis versos princesas, reyes, cosas imperiales, visiones de países lejanos o imposibles; ¡qué queréis!, yo detesto la vida y el tiempo en que me tocó nacer; y a un presidente de la República no podré saludarle en el idioma en que te cantara a ti, ¡oh Halagabal!, de cuya corte — oro, seda, mármol — me acuerdo en sueños . . ." It should not be difficult to understand Darío's frame of mind if we consider the cultural atmos-

---

[18] See Rufino Blanco-Fombona, *El modernismo y los poetas modernistas*, Madrid, 1929, pp. 165-166; Enrique Gómez Carrillo, *Obras completas de Rubén Darío*, Madrid, 1918, X, 219-220 and Leopoldo Lugones' prologue to *Prosas profanas*, México, 1919, pp. 16-17. Also consult Antonio M. de la Torre, "Consideraciones sobre la actitud político-social de Rubén Darío," *Revista Iberoamericana*, XIX (septiembre, 1954), 261-272 and Edmundo García Girón's essay "El modernismo como evasión cultural" *in La cultura y la literatura iberoamericana*, México, 1957, VII, 131-137. There comes to mind Dámaso Alonso's remark on the "cultismo" as an aspect of the flight from reality in *La lengua poética de Góngora*, Madrid, 1935, p. 116.

phere then. There was the feared imperialist threat of the United States. Add to this the growing prosperity that in Argentina and Uruguay reached many levels of society. Elsewhere, the economic progress, if not very marked, was nonetheless in evidence. "Reyes burgueses" seemed to be everywhere. The prevalent cultural standards, along with the rather impoverished state of the Spanish language, more than justified Darío's seeking a source of inspiration more likely to stimulate the creative process.[19]

Darío was hardly the first artist to admit to a lack of empathy with his environment. Horace, in his *Odes* 3.1.1 shouted, "Odi profanum volgus et arceo." Moreover, writers throughout the nineteenth century cried out against the materialism and the ugliness of the world about them. Who can help but recall Wordsworth's accusation that his contemporaries, concerned only with making and spending money, were killing their own souls? So, in "The World is too much with Us," he says:

> So might I, standing on this pleasant lea, . . .
> Have sight of Proteus rising from the sea;
> Or hear old Triton blow his wreathèd horn.

Better, says Wordsworth, to be a pagan believing in the divinities of Greece, for at least the Greeks could feel the beauty of the external world.

Physically, the nineteenth century landscape was undeniably ugly. As thriving mills darkened the sky with smoke and filled the air with soot, numerous distinguished men of letters agreed that they could only loathe the world in which they had to live. How could they be inspired to beauty and lofty ideals by what they saw around them?

[19] See Arturo Torres-Rioseco, *Vida y poesía de Rubén Darío,* Buenos Aires, 1944, pp. 195-202 concerning Darío's nationalistic feelings, as well as Professor Torres-Rioseco's *Casticismo y americanismo en la obra de Rubén Darío,* Cambridge, Mass., 1931. Enrique Anderson Imbert speaks of Darío's return to social and national themes in Rubén Darío, *Poesía,* ed. Ernesto Mejía Sánchez, México, 1952, pp. xxviii-xxx.

Mist clogs the sunshine.
Smoky dwarf houses
Hem me round everywhere;
    A vague dejection
Weighs down my soul.[20]

The increasingly industrialized cities that seemed to be surrounding them, along with the vulgar "cultural" tastes of their contemporaries, compelled them to look to other times and places, beautiful in and of themselves, and somewhat lovelier by their remoteness. Often, but not invariably, they turned towards ancient Greece and Rome. Rimbaud went to Java and then to Africa. Pierre Loti, among others, went to the Orient. Baudelaire was one of those who fled to the world of drugs. Still others found the Middle Ages appealing, but no one place was as satisfying to so many as the Greco-Roman world.

Some writers incorporated many exotic motifs into their works. The Parnassian leader Leconte de Lisle, sometimes described as a pure Hellenist or a reincarnated Greek, begins his *Poèmes antiques* (1852-1872) with accounts of Hindu legend before moving on to Greece. His *Poèmes barbares* (1862-1878) portrays Biblical antiquity, Phoenician, Scandinavian and Celtic history as well as medieval and modern times. Leconte de Lisle's disciple Heredia, in *Les trophées* (1893), is also inspired by diverse times and places ranging from Greek pre-history to Egypt and Japan.

V *The Impact of Azul . . .*

Darío, too, evoked many exotic climes in addition to the Greco-Roman. Beginning with *Azul . . .* we see a lexicon that is the result of a sensitive and meticulous search. Yet, the fame of *Azul . . .* was by no means instantaneous. In spite of Valera's studies on *Azul . . .*, which were published in *El Imparcial* in October of 1888, this book was not then well-

---

[20] Compare these lines from Arnold's "Consolation" with other verses from Wordsworth's "The World is too much with Us": "Great God! I'd rather be / A Pagan suckled in a creed outworn."

22

known in Spain; it was the Barcelona edition in 1907 that really made the Spaniards aware of *Azul* . . . .[21] Valera's keen observations, at times appreciative and at other times condescending, do not seem to indicate that he suspected the magnitude of the poetic revolution to be provoked by *Azul* . . . .

However, Darío was not unknown in Spain between 1888 and 1899, the time of his second trip there. He had published some of his poems in Spanish journals during his first visit to Spain in 1892. Basically, though, the official Spanish literary taste of the times ran along different lines. The astute Clarín dominated the scene and he was, around 1890, the most widely read critic. One of his first attacks on modernism dates back to 1893. Darío in turn accused him of not fully understanding *Azul* . . . :

> Yo no soy jefe de escuela ni aconsejo a los jóvenes que me imiten; y el ejército de Jerjes puede estar descuidado, que no he de ir a hacer prédicas de decadentismos ni a aplaudir extravagancias ni dislocaciones literarias.
>
> Clarín debe procurar lo que vale de las letras americanas. Un día escribió, sobre poco más o menos: '¿Qué tengo yo que saber de poetas americanos como de la gran China?' Estúdienos y así podrá apreciar justamente lo que hay de bueno entre nosotros. Y por un galicismo o un neologismo no condene una obra.[22]

Like Valera, who had earlier accused Darío of a "galicismo mental," Clarín, in a commentary on "Cosas del Cid," criticizes Darío for being too fond of "poesía comparada:" "Por Dios, Rubén Darío, usted, que es tan listo, y tan elegante . . . a la española, cuando quiere, déjese de esos 'galicismos internos,' que son los más perniciosos. ¿Para qué ese afán de ser extranjero?" (Díaz-Plaja, p. 48). But Darío, who never took an intensely personal attitude to the attacks upon him,

---

[21] So states Díaz-Plaja, *op. cit.,* p. 51, in contrast with Julio Saavedra Molina, who says that the 1888 and 1890 editions circulated freely both in Latin America and Spain. Díaz-Plaja further maintains that the second edition of *Prosas profanas* (Paris, 1901) was the one important to Spanish literature, not the first edition (Buenos Aires, 1896).

[22] Quoted by Díaz-Plaja, *op. cit.,* p. 47.

seemed to get the last word in a rather admirable summation of the polemic:

> El libro *Azul* . . . no tuvo mucho éxito en Chile. Apenas se fijaron en él cuando don Juan Valera se ocupara de su contenido en una de sus famosas *Cartas Americanas* . . . . Valera vió mucho, expresó su sorpresa y su entusiasmo sonriente —¿por qué hay muchos que quieren ver siempre alfileres en aquellas manos ducales?—; *pero no se dió cuenta de la trascendencia de mi tentativa.* Porque si el librito tenía algún personal mérito relativo, de allí debía derivar nuestra futura revolución intelectual. (Díaz-Plaja, p. 52)

After the publication of *Prosas profanas,* Darío was acclaimed the greatest poet in the language since Quevedo's death. This book abounds with luxurious and exotic details, drawn from all points of the compass, but with Versailles as the undeniable meridian.[23] There was, of course, the inevitable reaction against him that is synthesized in González Martínez's sonnet "Tuércele el cuello al cisne . . ." (1910). Darío's admirers were fascinated by his verbal facility, his wealth of literary allusions, his rich imagery and the rhythmical skill of his verse. His detractors, annoyed by his preciosity and love of the external world, labelled him "retórico" and thought him lacking in the intimacy and depth of Garcilaso, Quevedo and Bécquer. Yet he has something in common with these great poets; he left Spanish poetry different from the way in which he found it. Whatever the individual opinion may be, Darío's influence is undeniable. His impact was so great that almost any poem written in Spanish can be labelled *pre* or *post* Darío. In particular, we shall see how he distinguishes himself in his portrayals of the Greco-Roman world.[24]

[23] Pedro Henríquez Ureña in *Literary Currents in Spanish America,* Cambridge, 1945, p. 172, points out that the foreign trappings of Darío and his followers were really a disguise. Under that mask, we see the reappearance of wealth in Latin America. Although the romantics had little real experience with luxury, men like Darío actually had seen great prosperity. Versailles became a symbolic name for this new way of life in the now prosperous cities of Latin America.

[24] Editions used are Rubén Darío, *Cuentos completos,* ed. Ernesto Mejía Sánchez, México, 1950, and Rubén Darío, *Obras poéticas completas,* 6th ed., Madrid, 1949. Since the quotations are so numerous, they will be given within the text and will be designated respectively as *CC* and *OPC.*

CHAPTER II

"SMALL SKILL IN LATIN"

Darío himself made an important statement concerning his background in classical Greco-Roman literature. From his words in *Todo al vuelo* (1912) we again feel the impact of his relationship with the Jesuits: "He de insistir siempre en que los padres de la Compañía de Jesús fueron los principales promotores de una cultura que no por ser si se quiere conservadora deja de hacer falta en los programas de enseñanza actuales. Por lo menos conocíamos nuestros clásicos y cogíamos al pasar una que otra espiga de latín y aun de griego." The period of most intense Jesuit influence on Darío, 1878 to 1880, coincides with his acquiring a taste for mythological themes and motifs. The smattering of Latin acquired during those years with the Jesuits must have been precisely that. The Latin quotations in the few years following 1880 that are not textual are marked by elementary errors, proof enough of the depth and permanence of his early lessons in the classical languages. From the time that Darío wrote his first verses under the guidance of the Jesuits in 1879 to his return from El Salvador in 1883 there are various scattered classical allusions in his writings. Just a few are "celeste numen," "frente ceñida de laurel," "Júpiter Tonante," "náyades," "laurel," and "Juvenal" (EMS, pp. 250-251). Two conclusions can be drawn from the nature of these references. First, they most likely did not originate in the classical texts themselves or even in the translations that might have been available to Darío. The majority probably were inspired by Spanish neoclassic poetry, the favorite model of the Jesuits. Second, such references are frequent literary stylizations of the Greco-Roman world. They are easily obtained and could be repeated with precision by anyone with a good memory. However, the important point is that Darío's fondness for the classical, not always taken seriously by his audience, was well-rooted in his spirit during the earliest years of his literary formation, prior to his trip to Chile in 1886.[1]

Moreover, we are told in "Las humanidades de Rubén Darío" that Darío's interest in the classics broadened considerably as he approached maturity. Two events stimulated this interest in the years 1883-1886: the publication of the "Biblioteca Clásica" of Madrid and his studies at the Biblioteca Nacional under the devoted guidance of Modesto Barrios and Antonio Aragón. We know that Baráibar's translation of Anacreon in *Poetas líricos griegos,* published in the "Biblioteca Clásica" (1884), influenced Darío. (See *ninfa.*) But Darío mentions prior to 1886 other writers that did not appear in the "Biblioteca Clásica." Ovid is referred to frequently in his allusions to "est deus in nobis." Darío mentions Horace, both in the original and in the Burgos translation. "Don Francisco Javier de Burgos, el excelente traductor de Horacio," writes Darío in his study on Calderón published in 1884. He also mentions the works of Martial and Menander, an imitation of Anacreon by D. Hermógenes de Irisarri not spoken of by Baráibar in his *Poetas líricos griegos,* and the translations and epigraphs of the *Odas, epístolas y tragedias* of Menéndez y Pelayo. Darío had already imitated the latter in Nicaragua in *Epístolas y poemas* (1885).

At the Biblioteca Nacional, he was patiently guided in his readings by the director, D. Modesto Barrios. In 1885 Barrios's successor as director, D. Antonio Aragón, also succeeded Barrios as mentor. Darío, in his *Autobiografía,* states his indebtedness and admiration of Aragón, "nutrido de letras universales, sobre todo de clásicos griegos y latinos. Me enseñó mucho." It is in Darío's journalistic writings of this period that Mejía Sánchez sees evidence of Darío's deepened classical

---

[1] In short, "La lección, como siempre, no es inútil si hay alguien que sepa aprenderla: Nicaragua tuvo una vez un poeta, y, en cierta medida, también supo educarlo." Mejía Sánchez, *op. cit.,* p. 263.

knowledge. He quotes, for example, from Darío's article on Calderón, "no le aventajará Teócrito en intentos, sí Virgilio en epítetos." Quoting a comment of Darío's made in 1884 on Carnevallini's translation of Walker's *Historia de la Guerra de Nicaragua,* Mejía Sánchez further says that Darío's classical knowledge extended to historical texts: "El autor de la obra no es el narrador que copia como Herodoto ni escribe con el juicio de Tácito, ni compara como Plutarco."

We do not see, however, that this kind of statement by Darío is proof that he had a real knowledge of the pertinent classical historical texts. On the contrary, for both of these references, like others previously cited, appear to be rather general and readily accessible to a cultured person. They do not necessarily indicate a detailed awareness of the writers mentioned. After all, such general characteristics of an author's style are to be found in any number of secondary sources ranging from encyclopedias to histories of literature. However, this disagreement is only partial, for we have seen in the preceding pages a certain progress in Darío's knowledge of classical literature, aided by the various translations. It must be stressed that "name dropping" and general references do not indicate an actual or a deep acquaintanceship with a subject. We offer as evidence the first analysis of Darío's Latin quotations in the *Cuentos completos* and his poetic works beginning with *Azul* . . . . Before drawing further conclusions, it is necessary to look carefully at these quotations, which fall into three main categories.

I *Biblical Latin Quotations*

Some of Darío's Biblical quotations demonstrate a mingling of the sensual and the religious in a manner that recalls a type of French literature of which Baudelaire is representative. "Mel et lac sub lingua tua," from the Song of Songs iv. 11 is one of that kind. In the story "Palomas blancas y garzas morenas" (1888) Darío describes the effects of a first kiss: "¡Oh Salomón, bíblico y real poeta! Tú lo dijiste como nadie: *Mel et lac sub lingua tua*" (*CC,* 91). This quotation recurs in a similar context in "Que el amor no admite cuerdas reflexiones" (1896):

> Mi gozo tu paladar
> rico panal conceptúa,
> como en el santo *Cantar*:
> *Mel et lac sub lingua tua.* (OPC, 669)

In "Coloquio de los centauros" (1896) Odites, eulogizing Hipodamia, clearly recalls this verse which so gracefully expresses an amorous state: "Como una miel celeste hay en su lengua fina." In contrasting tone is Darío's poem "Ite, missa est" (1896), an "amorous Mass," a parody of the type popular in the fifteenth century that Menéndez y Pelayo termed "irreverencia y profanación."[2] This Latin expression is undoubtedly one of the many Darío knew from the ritual of the Church.

The opening lines of the Sequence in the Office of the Dead appear in "Madrigal exaltado" (1905) in a frivolous manner analogous to Darío's use of "Mel et lac sub lingua tua:"

> *Dies irae, dies illa!*
> *Solvet saeclum in favilla*[3]
> cuando quema esa pupila! (*OPC,* 732)

(In this poem, as well as in the following one, Darío uses *solvet,* a future tense, as if it were a present. If we assume he was unaware of this confusion of tenses, we have evidence of his limited Latin preparation.)[4] On the other hand, in

---

[2] Quoted by Marasso, p. 66, who points out a striking coincidence of lines between Darío's "Ite, missa est" and that of Suero de Ribera, whom Darío probably did not know.

[3] The authorship of this hymn is not certain. It has been attributed to Thomas de Celano, a Minorite friar of the fourteenth century. More commonly it is believed to have been written by Frangipani, Cardinal Malabrancia. See *Dictionary of Latin Quotations,* ed. H. T. Riley, London, 1859, p. 83.

[4] For other data on Darío's knowledge of Latin, see Mejía Sánchez, *op. cit.,* p. 249, where he points out that the opinions of Valle-Inclán and Osvaldo Bazil are not as contradictory as they first seem. Valle-Inclán claims only that Darío had perfect pronunciation, while Bazil denies him solid semantic and syntactic knowledge of the language. Also, J. B. Trend in *Rubén Darío,* Cambridge, England, 1952, pp. 10-11 as well as in his article *"Res metricae* de Rubén Darío" in the *Libro jubilar de Alfonso Reyes,* pp. 383-390, credits Darío with a tech-

"Santa Elena de Montenegro" (1907) this quotation figures in the Middle Ages' fearful vision of death, which Darío vividly re-creates in an atmosphere saturated with "el olor de muerte." The horrible effects of Christ's Crucifixion are graphically portrayed in a succession of terror-filled stanzas. The effect is intensified by the allusion to the same lines from the Mass for the Dead:

> La luna huraño humor destila
> en la tumba de la Sibila
> y *solvet seclum in favila* [sic]
> . . . .
> Hay pueblos de espectros humanos
> que van mordiéndose las manos.
> Comienzan su obra los gusanos. (*OPC*, 854)

It should be noted that Leconte de Lisle wrote "Dies irae" in *Poèmes antiques,* a melancholy reflection on the pagan beauty that was lost with the coming of Christ, and "Solvet seclum" in *Poèmes barbares.*

More numerous than Darío's Biblical-sensual quotations are the Biblical and liturgical ones associated with his fear of death. It is a terrified and repentant Darío who cries out in "Sum . . ." (1907):

> ¡Señor, que la fe se muere!
> Señor, mira mi dolor.
> *Miserere! Miserere!*
> Dame la mano, Señor . . .

The "Miserere" is the fiftieth Psalm; moreover, "Miserere nobis" occurs in every Mass. "Sum . . ." itself seems to recall St. Paul's letter to the Romans xi. 36: "Quoniam ex ipso, et per ipsum, et in ipso sunt omnia: ipsi gloria in saecula." "Sum . . ." is one of Darío's most anguished interrogations of the problem of being. From the abyss of his own fear and ignorance he cries out to the God that does not answer:

nical knowledge of the placing of accents in Latin verse that Darío could not have had. The numerous lapses of memory and basic errors we see in Darío's Latin do not support Trend's stand. For example, "tempestarii" in the story "Cuento de Pascuas" leaves us wondering exactly what Darío had in mind.

¡Señor, que la fe se muere!
Señor, mira mi dolor.[5]

In Darío's later years, when his fear of death is greater
than his interest in the "jardines versallescos" and "las ninfas
de carne y hueso," there is an awareness of the vanity of
mundane pleasures that struggles against the ever-present attraction to the world. In the "Dedicatoria" of the *Poema del
otoño* (1907), a grim reminder of the fleeting nature of
worldly joys is achieved by the insertion of the beginning of
the prayer for the dead:

El domingo de amor te hechiza:
mas mira cómo
llega el miércoles de Ceniza;
Memento, homo . . .

Darío would like to be strong enough to abandon these pleasures. He desires the peace and assurance of the monks he
knew in Mallorca, who, having abandoned the world, are prepared for death:

¡Ah! fuera yo de esos que Dios quería,
y que Dios quiere cuando así le place,
dichosos ante el temeroso día
de losa fría y *Requiescat in pace!* (*OPC,* 862)

This line is another reminiscence of the Mass for the Dead.
(It is clear from the rhyme of these verses that Darío used
the Spanish, not the Italian pronunciation of *pace.*) To describe
further the religious solitude and indifference to the world of

5 In this discussion of Darío's Biblical Latin quotations, the substantives
réquiem, oremus, ángelus and *paternoster* are not included in the text. They are
words admitted into Spanish and as such do not pertain directly to the problem
of analyzing Darío's Latin quotations. However, these words have a certain interest because of their connotation in the images involved. We are here concerned
with *réquiem* and *oremus.* So great is Darío's fear of death that he expresses
envy of the "osos misteriosos" in "Canción de los osos" (1913) in verses that
show an ambiguity of melancholy humor and tenderness. "Mas no el *requiem,*
ni el *oremus,* ni el responso del gangoso / chantre llegue a vuestro oído, / sabio
y suave oso." *Requiem* and *oremus* are recollections of the somber Mass for the
Dead. Neither the 1941 nor 1949 Aguilar editions has the accent on *requiem*
in "La canción de los osos," though the Mejía Sánchez edition does. However,
"Pax" contains *requiem* according to the latter and *réquiem* in the Aguilar
editions.

those monks he envies, Darío uses a fragment of Colossians ii. 20. St. Paul warns, "Wherefore if ye be dead with Christ from the rudiments of the world, why, as though living in the world, are ye subject to ordinances?" Darío inserts a fragment of "Si ergo mortui estis cum Christo . . ." in "La cartuja" (1907). These monks have triumphed over mundane complications:

> Que el *Mortui estis* del candente Pablo
> les forjaba corazas arcangélicas
> y que nada podía hacer el diablo
> de halagos finos o añagazas bélicas.

In spite of Darío's longing for peace and the promise of salvation, he remains uncertain.[6]

In "Spes" (1905) Darío's undeniable sincerity is striking. His hope for salvation is based on a Christ that he sees as an "incomparable perdonador de injurias." Undoubtedly, Darío is at this moment quite close to his kindred spirit, Paul Verlaine, who showed a similar intensity of emotion in so many of his desperate pleas to the Blessed Virgin. The word *spes* itself could be a recollection of Romans viii. 24: "Spe enim salvi facti sumus. Spes autem, quae videtur, non est spes: nam quod videt quis, quid sperat?" Hugo, too, uses *spes* as a title of a poem in *Les contemplations.*

Devout in a different way is Darío's other poem "Spes" from his *Lira póstuma.* Writing in commemoration of the

---

[6] One of Darío's most anguished poems is "La dulzura del ángelus." Prior to Darío the theme of the bells of the Angelus had acquired intimate poetic context in the nineteenth century. Millet paints this prayer time with the sound of invisible bells echoing through the fields. The *Revista Azul,* founded by Gutiérrez Nájera in 1884, published such notable poems as "Angelus Domini Ocaso" by Manuel José Othón and "Angelus" by Jesús E. Valenzuela. Mallarmé, in his sonnet "Le sonneur" did not give himself over to the sentimental emotion so beautifully suggested in the first stanza. Darío evokes something more profound than the mere ringing of bells in "La dulzura del ángelus" (1905), for it is the ringing of "campanas provinciales" when the traveler pauses to say his "Ave María." The whole air of calm is delicately captured in the opening lines: "La dulzura del ángelus matinal y divino / que diluyen ingenuas campanas provinciales" (*OPC,* 716). But the serenity is interrupted by an anguished lament that recalls the desolate emotion of "Sum . . .": "todos hechos de carne y aromados de vino / Y esa atroz amargura de no gustar de nada, / de no saber adónde dirigir nuestra prora."

death of a young girl, he says that the only consolation for those left behind is her rise to eternal life. He shows himself quite orthodox in his acceptance of the greater importance of the hereafter. Indeed Darío is quite far removed from the hedonistic spirit shown in his earlier works.

However, Darío, still not certain of his personal destiny, has found the answer to universal strife in "Pax" (1915):

> y contra el homicidio, el odio, el robo,
> Él es la Luz, el Camino y la Vida. (*OPC,* 1059)

(See "Ego sum lux.") The *pax* that Darío here describes is not a personal one, but rather his expression of his belief in the Divine Providence of God. In a distinctly different manner, Gutiérrez Nájera, Nervo and González Martínez each wrote a poem called "Pax Animae." On the other hand, it is in Don Quijote that Darío places his hope for mankind in "Letanía de nuestro señor Don Quijote" (1905). With complete faith in Don Quijote, and using terminology frequent in Church liturgy as a plea for Christ's intercession, Darío invokes the aid of Don Quijote. It is a conscious variation similar to others we shall see. In the "Letanía:"

> ¡Ruega por nosotros, que necesitamos
> las mágicas rosas, los sublimes ramos
> de laurel! *Pro nobis ora,* gran señor.

Although the liturgical sentence was certainly familiar to Darío, it is also interesting to note that "Ora pro nobis" was used by Hugo as an epigraph to "La prière pour tous," translated into Spanish by Bello as "La oración por todos."

Pater, the last Biblical reference concerning Darío's religious state, is not, like the others, an indication of his fear of death. In one instance *pater* prophesies the triumph of the Christian over the pagan in Darío. In a weird recollection of two diabolic "enanos como los de Velázquez," the poet cowers, terrified, as he watches one of them in a sacrilegious parody:

También fingía ser obispo y bendecía;
predicaba sermones de endemoniado enredo
y rezaba contrito *pater* y avemaría.[7] (*OPC*, 972)

"La fiesta de Roma" (1898) seems to be an instance of the levelling of Christian and pagan figures that we shall discuss at length in Chapter v. *Pater* is an epithet of Jupiter; he is in reality Jupiter-Christ. Speaking of Rome, Lucius Varus says, "Es la diosa dueña de la inmortalidad y de la victoria, favorecida directamente del Divus Pater Júpiter" (*CC*, 270).

The last group of Biblical Latin phrases ranges from a poem called "Charitas" to a proclamation of Darío's aesthetic creed in the words of St. John. These rather varied quotations seem to be largely a display of erudition, a tendency that first becomes most apparent in the Darío of *Prosas profanas*. In the story "Voz de lejos" (1896) there is a Biblical-erudite overtone in the use of a Latin word: "Ellas son trasunto de aquella visión del evangelista Juan, la cual tenía, sobre su cabeza, escrita la palabra *Misterium*."

In the "Canto a la Argentina" (1910) there is a conscious variation on the first line of the "Ave Maria:" "Ave, Argentina, vita plena!" Darío, in his fervor, seems almost to be giving a divine character to Argentina. Though in this poem there is an intermingling of eight and nine syllable lines, the latter predominates. Undoubtedly, Darío intended this Latin verse as a nine syllable one, for there is in Latin no synalepha as we would ordinarily have in a Spanish verse between *Ave* and *Argentina*. A further variation is that Darío substitutes *vita* for *gratia*. Hugo used as an epigraph to "A Madame Marie M." the uncorrupted line "Ave, Maria, gratia plena."

Darío's variations are not always so deliberate. In "Historia prodigiosa de la princesa Psiquia . . ." Darío proclaims that Jesus Christ will be honored "per infinita saecula saeculo-

---

[7] Here, Darío does not accent the underlined Latin word *pater* as he sometimes does *requiem*. His use of *paternoster* in the story "¿Por qué?" (1892) intensifies an irreligious tone by its own devout connotation. The figure of a corrupt priest is bitterly portrayed: "el cura es también aliado de los verdugos. Él canta su tedeum y reza su paternoster, más por el millonario que por el desgraciado."

rum," undoubtedly a quotation from memory of "per omnia saecula saeculorum," a phrase common in the Mass. A similar idea is expressed in Ephesians iii. 21: "Ipsi gloria in Ecclesia, et in Christo Iesu in omnes generationes saeculi saeculorum." In "La leyenda de San Martín" (1897) we find another obviously unconscious variation of a Latin quotation: "Beati Martini confesoris [sic] tui atque pontificis." The elementary spelling error strongly suggests that Darío was indeed quoting from memory. Of course, this mistake is still further indication of his limited knowledge of Latin. In full this quotation from the *Missale Romanum,* November 11, reads: "Deus, qui conspicis quia ex nulla nostra virtute subsistimus: concede propitius ut, intercessione beati Martini confessoris tui atque pontificis, contra omnia adversa muniamur." Darío proudly used a portion of these lines to document his own "San Martín, . . . confesor y pontífice de Dios" (*CC,* 268).

The sentence "Ignoramus et ignorabimus" in "El caso de la señorita Amelia" (1894), which Darío rather pompously uses to stress the fact that we know very little with certainty, strikes us as a simple paraphrase of Psalms 82.5: "Nescierunt, neque intellexerunt, in tenebris ambulant . . ."

Darío interestingly uses two Latin references to the Blessed Virgin, which are in sharp contrast with each other. One is in a historically faithful image, while the other is a mingling of Christian and pagan references. "Stabat mater dolorosa!" from the Mass for the Dead occurs in "Palimpsesto I," a vivid recollection of Calvary. Christ is described as "sublime y solitario." The pathos of the scene is artistically and powerfully culminated in two epigrammatic sentences: "María daba su gemido maternal, *Stabat mater dolorosa!"* (*CC,* 199). On the other hand, a poem in Darío's *Lira póstuma* shows a startling contrast in tone between the title and the poem proper. The title, "Mater pulchra," has a marked Christian connotation in that this is a frequent term of reference for the Blessed Virgin. However, the atmosphere of the poem is completely pagan, for

Es Grecia, es Roma. Clámides
y togas. Es el tiempo maravilloso. Es
el Partenón, el templo de Apolo, las Pirámides,
las glorias hechas ruinas que volverán después.

. . . .

Y con todo, la herida de su materno duelo
hace exclamar a César, inundado de cielo:
"¡Oh madre! ¡Oh madre! ¡Oh madre! ¡Oh dulce madre mía!"

(OPC, 999)

Darío wrote this poem in recognition of the death of the
mother of General J. Santos Zelaya. (See *clámide*.) The "O
Matre pulchra" from Horace, *Odes*, I, 16, 1, though possibly
familiar to Darío, does not seem to be an influence here. It
is more likely that he knew this phrase from any one of the
many hymns he must have heard where it is used to designate
the Blessed Mother.

Similar to the fidelity of description of Christ's mother
in "Palimpsesto I" is Darío's poem in honor of St. Vincent
de Paul. Darío's "Charitas" was probably inspired by Coppée's "Vincent de Paul," found in *Les récits et les élégies*. The
title is appropriately chosen, for St. Vincent de Paul is, in the
Catholic Church, the example par excellence of brotherly love.
St. Paul spoke words on charity that are now a platitude
among preachers. For example, in I Corinthians xiii. 1:
"Though I speak with the tongues of men and angels, and
have not charity, I am become as sounding brass, or a tinkling
cymbal." In I Corinthians xiii. 13: "And now abideth faith,
hope, charity, these three; but the greatest of these is charity."
These words are part of the liturgical vocabulary that Darío
learned from the pulpit. The same is true of "Salvete flores
martyrum!" in the "Elogio del ilustrísimo señor obispo de
Córdoba, fray Mamerto Esquiú, O.M." (1907). These words
are regularly heard in the Church on December 28.

In the semi-humorous setting of "Un sermón" (1892)
Darío describes the eloquence of the "preacher" by alluding
to God's command in Genesis i.3: "Fiat lux." In the story
we find, "Pensad en un himno colosal cuya primera soberana
harmonía comenzase con el fiat del Génesis" (*CC*, 178).

Gutiérrez Nájera wrote a poem called "Fiat Voluntas" as did Hugo in *Les rayons et les ombres.*

In contrast with the light tone of the Biblical allusion in "Un sermón" is the one in the somber and mysterious "La extraña muerte de Fray Pedro" (1913). Darío uses a quotation found in Psalms cxi. 10 as a judgment on Fray Pedro's insatiable thirst for knowledge: "initium sapientiae est timor Domini" (*CC,* 326).

Perhaps the most original of the images that Darío constructs with a Biblical quotation is in his proclamation in "Yo soy aquel . . ." (1905). "Ego sum lux et veritas et vita!" corresponds to John xiv. 6 except that Darío puts *lux* in place of *via*; but in John viii. 12, "Ego sum lux mundi." John xiv. 6 seems to be recalled almost literally in "Pax," but in the third person: "Él es la Luz, el Camino y la Vida" (*OPC,* 1059). In discussing poetic inspiration in "Yo soy aquel . . ." Darío defines his poetic creed in a magnificent metaphor that is the maximum point of aestheticism:

> Vida, luz y verdad: tal triple llama
> produce la interior llama infinita;
> el Arte puro, como Cristo, exclama:
> *Ego sum lux et veritas et vita!* (*OPC,* 688)

By contrast we might recall Hugo's "Homo sum" in the prologue to *Les contemplations.* Here, Hugo sees his work as "les Mémoires d'une âme." However, he considers his experience as "l'histoire de tous." Hugo's "Homo sum," in contrast with Darío's, does not imply his own individual personality inspired by the Divine, but declares the concept of all man as one. Still another variation of the two above passages from St. John is the epigraph to "Autumnal" (1888). This reads, "Eros, Vita, Lumen." However, *Eros,* Greek for *Love,* is a complete departure from these two passages from St. John, both of which contribute to this epigraph. As implied by *Eros,* the poem pertains to love. The fairy of love shows Darío, filled with "el ansia de una sed infinita," three things that are symbolic of each of these words. The stars symbolize

Lumen, the flowers *Vita* and "un bello rostro de mujer,"
Eros. Darío also wrote a poem called "Lumen-Gloria."

Darío is well within the romantic tradition in his equation of literature and religion.[8] In the "Proemio" of *El canto errante* he vigorously defends his innovations in the Spanish language with the use of Biblical and theological terminology. Never has he been closer to pedantry than when he says, "Los nuevos maestros se dedican, más que a luchar en compañía de las nuevas falanges, al cultivo de lo que los teólogos llaman *appetitus inordinatus propiae excellentiae.*" Darío is contemptuous of those who would cling to "vocablos sagrados" and clichés: "*Anatema* [sic] *sit* al que sea osado a perturbar lo convenido de hoy o lo convenido de ayer." The word order, as well as the spelling, indicates that Darío is quoting from memory. In I Corinthians xvi. 22: "sit anathema." Darío's weakness in Latin is even more apparent further on when he says: "Et verbum erat Deum." In John i. 1, which is recited in the Mass, we read: "In principio erat Verbum, et Verbum erat apud Deum, et Deus erat Verbum." Obviously, then, Darío's use of the accusative *Deum* rather than the nominative *Deus* is a syntactical, not a spelling error, based in part upon a confused mingling of "Verbum erat apud Deum" and "Deus erat Verbum."

II *Darío's Classical Quotations*

Darío's poem "Eheu!" (1907) seems to recall Horace's Odes, II, 14,1: "Eheu fugaces, Postume, Postume / labuntur anni, ..."[9] This poem is one of Darío's most terrified ponderings of life and death:

> ¿De dónde viene mi canto?
> Y yo, ¿adónde voy? (*OPC,* 802)

In "Pax" (1915) Darío contemplates the cruel spectacle of war and curses Pallas Athena-Science, whom he portrays

---

[8] See Professor Lida's preliminary study to the *Cuentos,* pp. xxx-xxxii.

[9] However, part of the last stanza of "Eheu!" clearly recalls Isaiah xl.3: "vox clamantis in deserto." In Darío, "Como en medio de un desierto / me puse a clamar."

as hating young men, "puesto que das las flechas y las balas" (*OPC,* 1058). In the midst of the description of the shooting he appropriately says, "Matribus detestata," which is taken from Horace, *Odes,* I, 1, 24.

Horace's *Odes,* II, 13 is cited in "Respecto a Horacio" (1893) in a surprise ending of the kind so typical in Darío's stories. Lucio Galo, who intended to kill Horace, admits, "El árbol no dió muerte al vate ilustre y él ha dejado al mundo los lindos versos que empiezan así: *Ille et nefasto te posuit die* . . . ." Darío's Latin quotations are certainly used with varying degrees of subtlety; here he seems to have strained a bit to allow himself the opportunity of inserting these lines, as appropriate as they may be in this instance.

The quotations from Virgil are more common. One in particular, "incessu patuit dea," is found often. These words are from the *Aeneid,* I, 405: "et vera incessu patuit dea . . . ." Venus disguised as a huntress is revealed to Aeneas and Achates by her graceful walk in one of the most celebrated episodes from this work. This incident is frequently recalled by Darío, directly or indirectly. In "Ésta era una reina" (1892) Amelia is described as walking so gracefully that "El *patuit dea* la denunciaría en todos lugares" (*CC,* 183). In his essay "Málaga" in *Tierras solares* (1904) the simple beauty of the women is eulogized: "Hay cuerpos que van rítmicamente andando con manera tal, que el *incessu patuit dea* os sale de los labios."[10] Darío's allusive references to this line have more grace and charm than his direct quotations, which come to constitute a rather worn image. In the portrait of a beautiful woman in "Acuarela" (1887) this Venus de Milo, dressed in the latest Parisian manner, is "gentil con sus gestos de diosa" (*CC,* 46). In the poem "Invernal" the poet would have his ideal with "bellos gestos de diosa" (*OPC,* 581). There are also other reminiscences of this meeting with Venus. Verses 402-404 read: "Dixit, et *avertens rosea cervice refulsit,* / Ambrosiaeque comae divinum vertice odorem / Spiravere:

---

[10] *Obras completas,* Madrid, 1917, III, 206. For other occurrences of this line in Darío, see the *Cuentos,* p. 183, note 4.

pedes vestis defluxit ad imos." (The italics are mine.) In the story "Palomas blancas y garzas morenas" (1888), "el vello alborotado de su *nuca blanca y rosa* era para mí como luz crespa" (*CC*, 89). In the same story we also find "su rostro color de canela y rosa." In "Marcha triunfal" (1905), "y bajo los pórticos vense sus rostros de rosa" (*OPC*, 707).

"Dic, quibus in terris inscripti nomina regum / nascantur flores . . ." in "En la batalla de la flores" is from Virgil's *Eclogues,* III, 106-107 and is inserted with reference to the "buenos días antiguos" when, as today, the beauty of Flora was celebrated on the lawns at Palermo. Another reference to Menalcas, who spoke these words, is made in the "Responso a Verlaine" (1896):

> Que si un pastor su pífano bajo el frescor del haya,
> en amorosos días, como en Virgilio, ensaya,
> tu nombre ponga en la canción.

"Iungamus dextras" is another Virgilian expression Darío uses. In the story "El último prólogo" Darío is taken to task by a young admirer for so freely writing hyperbolic praises in prologues: "Siquiera se contentase usted con imitar las esquelas huguescas: 'Sois un gran espíritu'. 'Iungamus dextras'. 'Os saludo'. ¡Pero no!" Darío goes far beyond comradeship, making promises of glory that are never realized. The fraternal connotation of this phrase occurs again in Darío's essay on Leconte de Lisle in *Los raros.* Leconte de Lisle, himself such an artist, was awed by Hugo's works: "Luego, fué a él, barón, par, príncipe, a quien el Carlomagno de la lira dirigiera este corto mensaje imperial y fraternal: 'Jungamus dextras.'"

"Patria, carmen et amor" is the epigraph to the story "Historia de un 25 de mayo" (1896); its content is summed up in these three words. The epigraph, to all appearances coined by Darío, could have been suggested by his readings of Horace and Virgil. For example, compare the familiar "Hic amor, haec patria est" from the *Aeneid,* IV, 347.

"Arcades ambo" in the "Epístola" to Madame Lugones (1907) is a clear recollection of Virgil, *Eclogues,* VII, 4-5:

. . . . . . Arcades ambo,
et cantare pares et respondere parati.

"Arcades ambo" happens to be the title of one of Verlaine's "Invectives," which Darío mentions in "El último prólogo" (1913). Darío's interest in this phrase was undoubtedly stimulated by this poem of Verlaine's.

There are but two direct quotations from Ovid, only one really certain. In "El último prólogo" it is said with reference to the mediocre poets that "Se creen poseedores de la llama genial, del deus . . ." (*CC,* 322). In Ovid's *De Arte Amandi,* III, 549, we read:

Est deus in nobis, et sunt commercia coeli;
Sedibus aetheriis spiritus ille venit.

Darío identifies as Ovidian the lines used as an epigraph to "Oda a Mitre" (1906). They are from the "Epicedion Drusi," often attributed to Ovid, which had inspired Garcilaso centuries before. Darío's poem "Ibis" may be a reminiscence of Ovid's "Ibis," although Juvenal's was perhaps a more significant influence.[11] That Darío did not have a firm grasp on his classical readings becomes even more apparent in his *España contemporánea.* Speaking of Valera's quotation from Lucretius in his study on *Azul . . .,* Darío says, "Aquel de Ovidio, si gustáis: '. . . medio de fonte leporum.'" Marasso feels it is unlikely that Darío could have forgotten the origin of these lines and suggests that perhaps it is an example of Cervantine irony on Darío's part. However, the numerous lapses of memory we have pointed out in Darío's Latin quotations do make this hypothesis improbable.

In "Las razones de Ashavero" (1893) there is what may be construed by some as a remnant of Darío's readings of classical historians. The eagle, who speaks in favor of monarchy, proclaims: *"Ave Caesar* es mi mejor salutación." In Suetonius V, 21, we find, "Ave, Imperator, morituri te salutant." Most likely Darío heard this common expression, which is bantered about in various forms. Then too, he could have

---

11 See Marasso, *op. cit.,* p. 274.

noticed it in one of his models. In Hugo, for example, "Ave, Caesar, morituri te salutant" is the epigraph to "La Vendée." These are allusions to the cry of the Roman gladiators on entering the ring, "Ave, Caesar, morituri te salutamus."[12]

The last two classical Latin words are not direct classical quotations in the same sense as the preceding ones. One of them, "pro domo mea," from the "Proemio" of *El canto errante* has a Ciceronian ring. The other, *salve,* was a word widely used in a solemn address to any revered object. In Virgil's *Georgics,* II, 173: "Salve, magna parens frugum, Saturnia tellus." In Horace's *Odes,* I, 32, 15, *salve* is used similarly. Moreover, this word is found frequently in the Spanish neoclassic poets and throughout the nineteenth century, in Leandro Fernández de Moratín, Quintana, Bello, Valera, and Menéndez y Pelayo.[13] In "Salutación del optimista" (1905), Darío, as an optimistic prophet, opens his address with dignity and solemnity:

> Ínclitas razas ubérrimas, sangre de Hispania fecunda,
> espíritus fraternos, luminosas almas, ¡salve!

In "Programa matinal" (1905) there is a pantheistic salute to the sun that is solemn with the use of *salve*:

> Claras horas de la mañana,
> en que mil clarines de oro
> dicen la divina diana.
> ¡Salve al celeste Sol sonoro! (*OPC*, 745)

III *Casual Latin Words*

Darío uses several single Latin words and phrases, most of them in common circulation among educated people. We have included them for the sake of completeness and, above

---

[12] John Bartlett, *Familiar Quotations,* 13th ed., Boston, 1955, p. 1009.

[13] Moratín is quoted in Federico Ruiz Morcuende, *Vocabulario de D. Leandro Fernández de Moratín,* Madrid, 1945, II, 1380. Manuel José Quintana, *Poesías,* Madrid, 1927, pp. 110, 203. Andrés Bello, *Colección de poesías originales,* Paris, 1870, p. 54. Juan Valera, *Obras completas,* Madrid, 1907, XII, 167. Marcelino Menéndez y Pelayo, *Edición nacional de las obras completas,* Santander, 1955, LXII, 62, 111. *Salve* is also a common liturgical term. Darío, however, does not use it in a liturgical setting.

all, to show that a detailed analysis reveals that the presence of numerous Latin words and quotations is by no means an indication of a strong classical formation.

"Hic iacet frater Petrus" is an inscription on a tombstone in "La extraña muerte de Fray Pedro" (1913). These inscriptions were especially common on the tombstones of clerics in the Middle Ages.

Darío uses "imperator" on two distinct levels. In "Febea" (1892) "La doncella oyó el canto del formidable 'imperator' . . . ." In this case it is Nero. On the other hand, in "La fiesta de Roma" (1898) the "soberbio Imperator" is Christ. However, in both cases "imperator" means "emperor" or "monarch," not "triumphant general." Christ is described as the *"Dux* eterno y supremo" in "Los tres astros" from the *Lira póstuma.*

Darío's delight in his own pseudo-erudition is perhaps the explanation of the peculiar title "Morbo Et Umbra" (1888), apparently another of Darío's coinages. Similarly, we can sense his stylistic pleasure in the story "En la batalla de las flores" (1893) as Apollo, poet turned businessman, confesses "inter nos" that he has not completely abandoned his poetic endeavors; they must not, however, interfere with his financial affairs.

Darío uses "In memoriam" as an epigraph to the poem "Margarita" (1896) and as the title of verses in honor of Bartolomé Mitre (1907). This Latin phrase, common in modern usage, is also the title of a poem by Gutiérrez Nájera written in 1879.

In the queries as to the best form of government in "Las razones de Ashavero" (1893) the sparrow boasts of knowing the merits of "habeas corpus." This is a legal term, which originated in the English system of law. It has since become the principal basis of United States and English citizens' protection from illegal detention by government officials. It also holds in some South American countries such as Argentina.

"Homo sapiens," the single species of which the various races of mankind are but varieties, is used sarcastically in "Arte y hielo" (1888) by the sculptor bewildered at the uncomprehending "homo sapiens de Linneo" (*CC*, 109).

In "Las razones de Ashavero" the poet, "como el ave de Júpiter, si hablaba latín en la tierra del yankee, era para exclamar: *E pluribus unum*" (*CC*, 215). This motto, originally on the title page of the *Gentleman's Journal*, January, 1672, was adopted as the motto for the seal of the United States on June 20, 1782. In "Salutación al águila" (1907) this motto is Darío's salute to the eagle and to the strength of the United States:

> *E pluribus unum!* ¡Gloria, victoria, trabajo!
> Tráenos los secretos de las labores del Norte. (*OPC*, 784)

Another motto, that of Paris, is fittingly employed in "France-Amérique" (1906):

> Et toi, Paris!, magicienne de la Race,
> Reine latine, éclaire notre jour obscur,
> Donnez-nous le secret que votre pas nous trace
> Et la force du *Fluctuat nec mergitur!* (OPC, 898)

In "Pax" Darío hopefully pays tribute to both France and Germany by proclaiming "Vivat Gallia Regina! Vivat Germania Mater!" These simple exclamations were evidently coined by Darío.

"Alma Mater" is a term the Romans applied to their favorite goddesses. The phrase has been extended to mean an institution with which someone has close contact, especially a college or university. It is in this latter sense that Darío uses "Alma Mater" in "Palas Atenea":

> Y así en el medieval momento,
> con su refugio transitorio
> el oculto laboratorio,
> el *Alma Mater* y el convento . . . (*OPC*, 1055)

In *Baladas y canciones* "Laetitia" is the title of a poem, each stanza of which begins with an enthusiastic "¡Alegría!", the Spanish translation of the Latin word.

At the outset of the study of Darío's Latin quotations, it was not suspected that the least numerous would be those from classical authors, nor that the Biblical and liturgical ones would be so abundant.[14] We rather expected that most of his Latin quotations would be classical in origin. After this critical examination, it stands out as highly significant that the only classical authors Darío quotes are Horace, Virgil and Ovid. Now it is quite true that Darío did, in his formative years, enrich his classical background by reading, to some extent, famous classical writers either in the original or in such translations as those of Francisco Javier de Burgos, Menéndez y Pelayo, Baráibar and "Ipandro Acaico's" *Poetas bucólicos griegos* and *Odas de Píndaro*.[15] Yet, considering how Darío loved to display this kind of knowledge, it is logical to assume that he would have quoted from a wider range of classical authors if he were so able. It is of further significance that his quotations from Horace, Virgil and Ovid are, for the most part, those

[14] These facts were first observed and studied in detail in an earlier work of mine. See Dolores Ackel Fiore, *Greco-Roman Elements in the Vocabulary of Rubén Darío*, unpub. Ph.D. thesis, Radcliffe, 1958, typewritten. Gonzalo Sobejano, in *El epíteto en la lírica española*, Madrid, 1956, pp. 434-438, discusses the value of the liturgical term *eucarístico* in such poems of Darío's as "Blasón" and "Para una cubana." L. B. Bucklin, in "Some Spanish Words Derived from the Roman Liturgy," *Hispanic Review*, XXV (Jan., 1957), 50-62, makes a statement that I endorse: "The latter, [ecclesiastical language] generally betraying itself by a more or less pure Latin form, may come from several sources, but the most important is the liturgy itself. The physical presence of the people at Mass brings them into direct oral contact with the language of the church, and it would be strange indeed if they failed to remember some of the words and phrases they hear during the service." More recently, Edmundo García Girón, in "La adjetivación modernista en Rubén Darío," *NRFH*, XIII (1959), 345-351, speaks of the many associations Darío arouses by the use of terms such as *eucarístico*. See also Hermana Mary Avila, C.S.J., "Principios cristianos en los cuentos de Rubén Darío," *Revista Iberoamericana*, XXIV (enero-junio, 1959), 29-39. Indeed, one could do a fascinating study of the countless hagiographic and patristic references in Darío to give even further proof of his religious culture. The direct quotations herein involved are but one indication of that culture.

[15] Mejía Sánchez, *op. cit.*, p. 261, informs us that early in 1886 Darío began reading Pindar, though he does not textually cite him. Darío must have known "Ipandro Acaico's" translation of Pindar in the "Biblioteca Clásica," vol. LVII, for on speaking of the *Poetas bucólicos griegos*, Darío mentions other great ancient works translated by "Ipandro Acaico." As of 1886 the latter had published only *Odas de Píndaro* and *Poetas bucólicos griegos*. Darío then obviously knew D. José Ignacio Montes de Oca y Obregón's translation of Pindar in the "Biblioteca Clásica." This data, then, considerably predates Marasso's assertion, p. 233, that since Darío followed the work of the Roman School of Moréas, he was therefore a reader and admirer of Pindar.

that would be known to a cultured person with a basic Latin training. Therefore, the wide diffusion among cultured people of these quotations, plus the fact that of Darío's Latin quotations, the classical are the least common in his works from 1888 on, gives us valid reason to conclude that he possessed a decidedly limited knowledge of a small and very well-defined group of classical authors.

Moreover, it is doubtful that these quotations are reminiscences of his early readings. In all probability, Darío returned, under the stimulus of his French readings, to the basic classical texts with which he had been familiar as a youth. His accuracy in his classical quotations, in contrast with his Biblical and liturgical recollections, is convincing proof that he was not quoting from memory. Undoubtedly he had the appropriate texts, and possibly a dictionary of classical quotations, close at hand. Darío would have preferred us to think these quotations were spontaneous, but they are not usually inserted with enough ease to assure us that such was the case. It is noteworthy, too, that Darío rarely identified his assorted Latin quotations as did, for example, Banville, Laprade and Samain. Darío was proud, both of his talent and his knowledge. It was not always with a wink that he displayed his learning.

The inaccuracies in his Biblical and liturgical quotations indicate not only a limited mastery of the Latin language, but also a self-assurance on Darío's part. That he had heard several of these expressions frequently in church is now apparent; yet, he makes basic errors. It is surprising that he did not avail himself of a missal and a Bible[16] for the same reason that he must have thumbed through certain familiar classical texts. Apparently he did not feel the need of checking on himself in this area. It is not extraordinary, in view of Darío's own remarks on his religious upbringing, to find these expressions from the ritual of the Roman Catholic Church in his works.

[16] Darío did read the *Bible*. See Arturo Torres-Ríoseco, *Rubén Darío, Antología Poética*, Berkeley, 1949, p. xxxiii and Marasso, *op. cit.*, p. 3, who says: "La leía comúnmente en la traducción de Cipriano de Valera, y, en los últimos años, en el texto latino de la Vulgata." Similar testimony is given by Mejía Sánchez, "Las humanidades," p. 249.

(See note 14.) It does, however, seem noteworthy that so many of these liturgical references pertain to death, the fear of which was a constant and mounting preoccupation with Darío.

Apart from the influence of Darío's early religious experience, other factors must be taken into account to explain his use of Latin phrases. Hugo is the first among Darío's modern French models in whom there is a marked tendency for using numerous Latin words and quotations. A few examples are "Nox," "Patria" and "Ultima verba" in *Les châtiments*; in the fourth book of *Les contemplations*, "Veni, Vidi Vixi" and "Mors." Hugo was a good Latinist as were most of the others; the Lycée of that period emphasized classical studies. This phenomenon persists throughout nineteenth-century French literature, in Gautier, Laprade, Leconte de Lisle, Baudelaire, Banville, Sully Prudhomme, Daudet, Coppée, Heredia and Samain. However, the significance of this use of Latin varies with the author. In the last half of the nineteenth century the interest in Rome, as well as in Greece, was of a more intellectual nature, part of the quest for historical exactness. That this is a generalization becomes apparent when we consider the Latin liturgical phrases used so conspicuously by Baudelaire, Coppée and Verlaine. We have something quite distinct, for these expressions are part of an intimate poetry marked by a struggle between the sensual and the spiritual. In Baudelaire we find "De profundis clamavi" and "Franciscae meae laudes" in "Spleen et idéal." In Coppée we read "Benedicat vos omnipotens Deus," "Oremus," "Pater et Filius" and "Et Spiritus Sanctus" in "La bénédiction" from his *Poèmes modernes*. In Verlaine's *Liturgies intimes* there are such poems as "Asperges me," "Gloria in excelsis," "Credo" and "Agnus Dei."

There are countless other examples of Latin words and quotations in Darío's French models. Here is a sampling. In Gautier's *Émaux et camées* (1852) there is a poem entitled "Caerulei Oculi" in addition to the widely diffused "Pater" and "Ave" in "Coquetterie posthume." Laprade wrote "Sunium" and "Alma Parens," the latter clearly a reminiscence of Horace. Laprade also quotes Julius Caesar in *Questions d'art et de morale.* Latin quotations abound in Banville, who usually identifies his source. In *Les cariatides* (1842) the Latin epigraphs to "Phyllis" and "Le stigmate" are from Virgil and the Apocalypse respectively. In *Les stalactites* (1846) there are several epigraphs from Horace, Virgil and Ovid, all identified by Banville. In "Carmen I" he quotes from Horace. In "La femme aux roses," "La fontaine de jouvence" and "Idylle" the quotations are from Virgil. In "Ovide" appropriately enough it is upon Ovid that Banville draws. Moreover, in *Les princesses* Banville documents his epigraphs to "Pasiphaé" and "Andromède" in Virgil and Ovid respectively. The epigraph to "Messaline" is labelled Tacitus.

Daudet uses several Biblical and liturgical Latin words. A few are "Oremus" in "Miserere de l'amour" as well as in "Les trois messes basses" and "L'élixir du révérend père Gaucher," where Daudet also uses "Pater Noster" and "Oremus, Domine." "Les trois messes basses" is rich in other liturgical expressions such as "Credo," "Pater," "Ite, missa est" and "Deo gratias." In Samain there is a tragic "De profundis" in one verse of "Vieilles cloches" and an epigraph to "Destins" that he identifies as Virgilian. Similar expressions occur in Sully Prudhomme's *Les solitudes* (1869). In "La grande chartreuse" "miserere" is used. "Dies irae" appears in "Le dernier adieu," and "Angelus" and "Ave Maria" are used in "Le missel." In *Les vaines tendresses* (1875) there is a poem entitled "Sursum corda" and in *Les épreuves* (1866) one called "Homo sum."

However, without denying the influence of Darío's French models, it has to be said that certain nineteenth-century Spanish authors Darío knew also used Biblical, classical and commonplace Latin words and quotations. (Needless to say, the Latin tradition in Spanish literature could be traced back many centuries.) Valera used an abundance of Latin epigraphs and inserts. In his novel *Genio y figura* the epigraph is from Lucretius. In the poems "La resurrección de Cristo," "Plegaria" and "A Cristóbal Colón" we find respectively "Et dilexerunt homines magis tenebras quam lucem," "Amor vult esse sursum (De imit. Christi)" and "Et vidit Deus quod esset bonum." In Valera's "Trozos del Fausto" we find "Dies irae, dies illa." Valera also wrote a poem called "Confiteor Deo" that shows the influence of Coppée. In Bécquer's *Leyendas* there is a variety of Biblical expressions. In "Maese Pérez el organista" and in "La corza blanca" there is "Pater Noster;" in "Tres fechas," "Dies irae, dies illa!" and "De profundis clamavi a te!" In "El miserere" there are, as one might well expect, many references to the "Miserere." In Zorrilla's poem "Toledo" there is also an allusion to the "terrible *Miserere.*" Of course, there are numerous Latin phrases and quotations in Menéndez y Pelayo's works. To name but a few, "Ad usum scholarum," "Otium Divos," "ne quid nimis," "Carpe diem" and "Rectius vives" in the "Epístola a Horacio."

The fondness for Latin words is also seen in some of the pre-modernists. However, the usage is most pronounced in Gutiérrez Nájera (1859-1895). The following are some of his poems with Latin titles: "Fiat voluntas" in *Primeras poesías* (1875-1881), "Sicut nubes, quasi navis, velut umbra" in *Trovas de amor* (1875-1880), "In memoriam" in *Otros poemas juveniles* (1877-1881), "Resurrexit!" in *Caminos del viento* (1880-1883), "Ignota Dea" in *Ala y abismo* (1884-1887), "Tristissima Nox" also in *Ala y abismo* and "Non omnis moriar" in *Odas breves* (1893). Actually, the "galicismo mental" attributed to Darío had manifested itself earlier in Gutiérrez Nájera, who was also acquainted with Hugo, Lamartine, Musset, Gautier, Baudelaire, Coppée and Verlaine.

We see, then, that Darío had models in Spanish as well as in French literature for the use of Latin words and quotations. However, in his modern readings, the Biblical quotations with a sensual connotation seem primarily a French characteristic. Although Darío's youthful religious education cannot be discounted in explaining his many Biblical and liturgical quotations, this literature in France weighed heavily on those particular Biblical phrases Darío used in a sensual setting.

Chapter III

"AND STILL LESS IN GREEK"

Many of the leading nineteenth century writers were well-read classical scholars. Tennyson could recite all of Horace's odes from memory. Arnold and Swinburne considered reading Greek and writing poetry interdependent activities. Robert Browning was as much at home in Greek and Latin as in French and Italian. Among those that more directly concern us, Leconte de Lisle spent many years trying to perfect his Greek.[1] He even published translations of several classical works: *Odes anacréontiques* (1861), *Iliade* (1866), *Odyssée* (1867), *Hésiode* (1869), *Eschyle* (1872), *Horace* (1873), *Sophocle* (1877) and *Euripide* (1885). The Parnassian re-creation of ancient times had as its basis many complex reasons.[2] It was, though, part of the quest for historical exactness. The historical perspective that had in part been created by Gibbon, Winckelmann, Wood and Wolf spread and deepened in the nineteenth century. New history books were written. Vast historical paintings were produced. In plays on historical subjects care was taken to see that the details were authentic.

Leconte de Lisle stands out as one of those who wrote with a good historical sense. His penchant for exactness, coupled with his love of Greece, led him to reject the Roman names of the gods and goddesses in favor of the less commonly known Greek ones. His use of these designations, as well as

[1] Concerning Leconte de Lisle's knowledge of Greek and the accuracy of his translations, see Henri Peyre, *Louis Ménard, 1822-1901,* New Haven, 1932, pp. 480-490.

[2] Indispensable sources for a discussion of this point are two of Prof. Peyre's books: *Louis Ménard* and *L'influence des littératures antiques sur la littérature française moderne,* New Haven, 1941. Also see Pierre Martino, *Parnasse et Symbolisme,* Paris, 1925.

such spellings as *Héraklès,* was so controversial that just about everybody had an opinion on the merits of such a practice. As a matter of fact, Leconte de Lisle was not the first to distinguish the gods in this fashion. Goethe had earlier transliterated the proper Greek names in *Achilleid.* In French Thalès Bernard was the first to employ this technique. Likewise, Victor de Laprade, who was very knowledgeable concerning ancient Greece, dared to give certain gods their Greek names as did Louis Ménard. In "Éleusis" (1844) Laprade spoke of *Zeus, Hermès* and *Artémis,* among others. In his *Questions d'art et de morale* he frequently quoted in Greek.

Ménard was but one of the many who staunchly defended Leconte de Lisle's orthography: "Dans les *Poèmes antiques,* Leconte de Lisle a cherché à nous montrer les Grecs comme ils étaient et à les faire parler comme des Grecs."[3] R. Fath pays homage to Leconte de Lisle's scrupulous exactness, claiming "C'est le respect de la vérité qui lui fit adopter l'orthographe originale des noms propres."[4] Georges Noël argues that the Greek names "nous semblent assez propres à donner à la poésie une couleur plus franche et plus nettement locale."[5] Estève maintains that Leconte de Lisle's meticulous attention to the names of the divinities was indispensable to distinguishing them from their Roman counterparts with whom they had too long been confused.[6] Desonay defends such transliterations from an aesthetic viewpoint, stating that for those who love the past, as did Leconte de Lisle, the artifice of such orthography as *Aphrodite* awakens a fresher, more poetic image than *Venus;* likewise, *Héraklès* contains more of the primitive myth than *Hercule.* It seems that Leconte de Lisle, as part of his quest for historical exactness, sought to re-create the vigor and harshness of the original primitive myth by transliterating as he did.

[3] Fernand Desonay, "Le rêve hellénique chez les poètes parnassiens," *Revue de Littérature Comparée,* L (1928), 266.

[4] R. Fath, *L'influence de la science sur la littérature française dans la seconde moitié du XIXe siècle,* Lausanne, 1901, p. 63.

[5] Georges Noël, "La poésie impersonnelle et M. Leconte de Lisle," *Revue Contemporaine,* LXXV (1870), 665.

[6] Edmond Estève, *Leconte de Lisle,* Paris, [1923?], p. 106.

Similarly, Th. Gautier believed that by using, for example, the *k* in the name Chiron, Leconte de Lisle succeeded in producing an effect "plus farouche." Gautier adds that there are other advantages:

> Ce sont là sans doute des détails purement extérieurs, mais qui ne sont pas indifférents. Ils ajoutent à la beauté métrique par leur harmonie et leur nouveauté; leurs désinences inusitées amènent en plusieurs endroits des rimes imprévues, et dans notre poésie, privée de brèves et de longues, c'est un bonheur qu'une surprise de ce genre; l'oreille qui attend un son aime à être trompée par une résonance d'un timbre antique.[7]

Gautier concludes that the restoral of Greek names gives to Leconte de Lisle's works the over-all air of "un temple d'ordre dorique."

On the other hand, we have those negative or middle of the road attitudes. Ferdinand Brunetière first says that Leconte de Lisle's literal spelling was "un peu puéril," although he hastens to add that his work is "incomparable de couleur."[8] Fernand Calmettes, attacking the resultant phonetic difficulties, concludes, "Rien n'est plus spécieux et d'une prétention d'exactitude plus illusoire que le décalque des noms propres."[9] In a similar protest, Gustave Planche sees not precision, but confusion in Leconte de Lisle's *Héré* for the Greek *Hêrê* and in his *Hélios* for *Hêlios*. Moreover, Planche criticizes him for speaking of "le jeune Hélios" rather than "Phoibos." The latter is the word Homer used to designate the god, while *Hêlios* refers to the sun.[10] (Darío uses both forms equivalently.)

Other Parnassians, following Leconte de Lisle, were involved in this reform, though not to such an extent. In Anatole France and Heredia there is an occasional *Artémis, Hécaté* or *Séléné*. Heredia, usually such a faithful disciple of Leconte de Lisle, did not completely adopt the Greek terminology. In fact,

---

[7] Théophile Gautier, *Histoire du Romantisme,* Paris, 1874, p. 332.

[8] Ferdinand Brunetière, *Essais sur la littérature contemporaine,* Paris, 1896, p. 222.

[9] Fernand Calmettes, *Leconte de Lisle et ses amis,* Paris, 1902, pp. 325-328.

[10] Gustave Planche, "La poésie en 1853," *Revue des Deux Mondes,* III (1853), 1192-1215.

Heredia's names show an almost classic discretion; *Aphrodite* appears with or without an accent on the *e* according to the needs of the rhyme. Rémy de Gourmont sees Heredia's conservative orthography as proof of his good taste, unlike the "facile érudition mythologique" that, he says, makes some of Leconte de Lisle's poems unreadable.[11]

Banville was very much influenced by Leconte de Lisle's preference in this area. In "L'exil des dieux" we find assembled, among others, *Zeus, Apollon, Aphroditè, Athènè, Hèrè, Dionysos* and *Hèphaistos.* In "La cithare" there is a veritable mythological parade, with a distinct leaning towards the Greek names of the divinities: *Zeus, Hèra, Ploutôn, Poseidôn, Hermès, Arès, Perséphonè* and *Kronos.* The Greek *k* appears again in *Hèraklès* in "Le festin des dieux." There are other apparent influences of Leconte de Lisle on Banville. He quotes Hesiod's *Theogony* in the original in "Clymène." Elsewhere, as in "Ariane," he avails himself of Leconte de Lisle's translation of Hesiod. Undoubtedly, though, Banville's motivation for the use of Greek names was decidedly distinct from that of Leconte de Lisle, who was interested primarily in the intellectual aspect of Greece. With Banville, it was largely an admiration of Greece as a symbol of beauty. Professor René Jasinski has appropriately characterized Banville's fondness for the classical world: "Il ne cherche pas les éruditions auxquelles s'astreindra bientôt le Parnasse, mais seulement la lumière, la grâce des noms et des formes, une souriante irréalité donnant à l'amour toute sa douceur . . . ."[12]

Darío's attitude towards Leconte de Lisle's transliterations was decidedly positive, judging from his own statement in his essay "Leconte de Lisle" in *Los raros:* "Conservaba la ortografía de los idiomas antiguos y así sus obras tienen a la vista una aristocracia tipográfica que no se encuentra en otras."[13] For the most part, Darío is himself a conformist in his spelling. He uses, for example, *Hérakles* in "Coloquio de los centauros,"

11 Desonay, *op. cit.,* p. 411.
12 René Jasinski, *Histoire de la littérature française,* Paris, 1947, II, 574.
13 Darío, *Obras,* VI, 43.

"Al rey Oscar" and "A Francia." *Herakleo* also appears in the "Coloquio." At times, too, we find a *th* that is startling in modern Spanish where the phonetic has triumphed. Although Darío's transliterations were inspired to a large extent by his admiration for the "noble" and primitive effect of Leconte de Lisle's orthography, there had been a tradition of erudite spelling in Spanish that Darío surely knew. The Academy had once defended that orthography, though for reasons quite distinct from those of Leconte de Lisle and Darío. Since the Spanish tradition cannot be discounted in appraising Darío's innovations, a brief presentation of that idea is quite in order.

The vague Latinistic current that is apparent since the origin of the Spanish language grew with the writings of "mester de clerecía." This tendency gathered strength in the fifteenth century with the triumph of humanism, for the humanists developed the idea of the Latin ancestry of Spanish, Portuguese, Italian and French. Consequently, there was a rivalry among these languages to resemble most closely their mother tongue. This competition explains the profusion then of such Latinized spellings as *ph, th, ch* and *y*. With the advent of printing in Spain, there was an awareness of the need for regulating the orthography. Antonio de Nebrija was the first to attempt to systematize Spanish orthography. The basic principle he followed was that of phonetism. Nebrija stated, in a paraphrase of the Quintilian principle, "assí tenemos de escrivir como pronunciamos: i pronunciar como escrivimos: por que en otra manera en vano fueron halladas las letras."[14] The criterion of Quintilian and Nebrija is well supported in the sixteenth century among such continuators of Garcilaso as Ambrosio de Morales, Francisco de Figueroa and Herrera.

The etymological principle, applied with flexibility from the beginning and with a certain amount of insistence since the fifteenth century, was formulated with real vigor in the seventeenth century by Juan de Robles. Robles is but one

---

[14] Andrés Bello, *Estudios gramaticales,* Caracas, 1951, p. xxvii. The excellent and very comprehensive prologue is by Professor Ángel Rosenblat. Other quotations from this source will be given in the text.

example of those who maintained that preservation of etymological spelling gave an air of aristocracy to certain words. In his *Censura de la ortografía* (1629) he says, "Las grafías etimológicas son como títulos antiguos de nobleza, de limpieza de sangre, de honores y bienes . . . ." (It was on different grounds, as we have seen, that Leconte de Lisle and his admirers defended the *k* and *th* of their transliterations.) Even less flexible in his preference for the etymological principle was Bravo Grajera. The basic idea of his *Breve discurso* (1634) is that "sin duda alguna es necesario conservar los vestigios de la antigüedad." Therefore, he argued that words of Greek origin should be written with *ph, th* or whatever the case might be according to the word.

Although Spanish orthography remained largely a matter of personal opinion until the nineteenth century, the desire for linguistic and orthographic regulation led to the formation of the Spanish Academy in 1713. In the earliest stages the Academy proclaimed itself the champion of etymological spelling. In reality the Academy was far from applying this principle consistently. This theoretical etymological stand can be traced, in part, to the viewpoint of the French Academy. The preface of the *Dictionnaire de l'Académie* (1694) says, "L'Académie s'est attachée à l'ancienne Orthographe receüe parmi tous les gens de lettres, parce qu'elle ayde à faire connoistre l'Origine des mots." In the light of its own experience and with the intention of self-correction, the Spanish Academy published its *Orthographia* in 1741. Etymology, according to the Academy, is no longer the fundamental and decisive criterion. Pronunciation should be a guiding principle. In short, the Academy was captivated by the Horatian principle of common usage. However, it must be noted that etymology was still very important to the Academy. The reason was that since Latin wrote words such as *philosophia* and *charitas* to indicate their noble genealogy, Spanish should do the same. For the most part, though, each new step the Academy took was towards phonetism. In 1754 the second edition of the *Ortografía de la lengua castellaña* appeared. The title, without the *th* or *ph,* is evidence of the abandonment of etymological spelling. The Academy's various orthographic reforms were finally incorporated into the 1817 *Diccionario.* In less than a century the Academy passed from its rigid etymological stand to the acceptance of Quintilian and Nebrija's principle.

The Academy, however, had not succeeded in ending orthographic anarchy. Throughout the eighteenth century and during the first part of the nineteenth, there was an active extra-academic movement. In 1728 Antonio Bordazar de Artazu published his *Ortografía española,* prefaced with a letter by Gregorio Mayáns y Siscar. Though the dictionary of the Academy had appeared two years earlier, Mayáns maintained that the nature of letters was fixed and their combination invariable. Personal feuds aggravated the whole polemic. Feijóo eulogized Bordazar's work until Feijóo accepted the erroneous opinion then circulating that attributed authorship to his enemy Mayáns. Because of Feijóo's initial eulogy of the work, Salvador José Mañer revised in 1730 his own traditionalistic work done five years earlier in such a way that he attacked Bordazar. Gradually, though, the authors of grammars and treatises on orthography accepted the Academic criterion. Bello and Sarmiento's attempt at reform in the nineteenth century was prompted by a genuine concern for facilitating the education of Spanish-Americans. It was not a mere rebellion against Academic authority. However, the issue was settled by order of Queen Isabel in 1844. The academic orthography was imposed upon the educational system. Later, Unamuno, who believed that Bello's rejection of accepted norms was a healthy state of mind, preached deference to the academic regulation: "Creo lo más eficaz para destruir la ley empezar por acatarla; el aceptar algo como mal necesario es el principio de su eliminación. Resignación, pues, a la actual ortografía, pero resignación activa" (Rosenblat, p. cxxxv).

Darío could not accept the rigidity Spanish was submitted to in the nineteenth century. The simplification of the orthography, to him, had deprived certain words of their aesthetic value. Hence, his admiration for the "aristocracia tipográfica" of Leconte de Lisle. In nineteenth century Spanish usage, Darío was preceded in this taste by Menéndez y Pelayo, the first one to bring the Greek names of the gods to Spanish, according to Marasso. We see these names commonly in his translations of Aeschylus and Theocritus. In "Sáficas I" (1875) he uses *Eros* and *Afrodita*. Moreover, the etymological *y* he employs is also to be found in Gutiérrez Nájera's ode "A Dyonisos" and in Casal's "Venus Anadyomena." In short, Darío's quest for freshness is manifested not only in the introduction of new poetic motifs, but also in his language.[15] In his prose and poetry there are numerous Hellenisms such as *peplo* and *liróforo*. He used words from various foreign languages, *staccati* and *sportswoman*, and, of course, the Latin words already discussed. Of particular interest are certain other linguistic devices of his: Greek transliterations, words that imitate the morphology of Greek patronymics and his fondness for the Greek names of such objects as *ánfora* and *canéfora*.[16]

I *Greek Transliterations*

Anagké. The Greek word, first used in the *Iliad*, 6, 458, means force, constraint or necessity and is frequently personified by poets to mean Fate. Darío wrote a poem "Anagké" that, according to Juan Valera, is a blasphemy against God.[17] Professor Lida, in his preliminary study to the *Cuentos*, is the first to indicate the likely influence of Hugo on the poem by Darío. Moreover, Professor Lida points out that the same desolate vision of the world is apparent in "El Dios bueno:" "pero aún están vivos los reproches de Valera al poema de

[15] Even those in the "Generación del 98" who were hostile to Darío's poetry considered him an innovator. See Jerónimo Mallo, "Las relaciones personales y literarias entre Darío y Unamuno," *Revista Iberoamericana*, IX (febrero de 1945), 61-72 and John E. Englekirk, "El hispanoamericanismo y la generación del 98," *Ibid.*, II (noviembre de 1940), 321-351.

[16] For a discussion of these and other stylistic devices in Darío, see Erwin K. Mapes, *L'influence française dans l'oeuvre de Rubén Darío*, Paris, 1925, pp. 37-138. Mapes discusses the themes, vocabulary and style of *Azul . . .*, *Prosas profanas* and *Cantos de vida y esperanza*.

[17] Marasso, *op. cit.*, p. 327 synthesizes the interpretations of this poem.

Azul . . ., y Rubén se apresura a aclarar en el subtítulo: 'Cuento que parece blasfemo pero que no lo es' " (*CC,* lix). Specifically we find that chapter iv, book VII of Hugo's novel *Notre Dame de Paris* (1831) is called "'ANÁTKH." Moreover, in "Le poëme du jardin des plantes" from *L'art d'être grand-père,* Hugo writes, "La Providence un peu servante d'Anankè." Darío is obviously uncertain of his Greek judging from the variations on this word. In the poem "Anagké" the misplaced accent could be the influence of Hugo's form in "Le poëme du jardin des plantes." Later in "Rojo" (1892) the word is stressed correctly but follows the French spelling: *ananke.* However, in the "Canto a la Argentina" (1910) Darío curiously reverts to the incorrectly accented *Ananké,* most surely the influence of Hugo's later form both in spelling and accent.

Kitón. This was a garment worn only by men as testified to in the *Odyssey* 15, 60. In later times we hear of two kinds, the Ionian and the Doric.[18] The Ionian was, like the Homeric one, made of linen. However, it was worn by women as well as men according to Herodotus 1.8, 5.87. It is this one that seems to figure in "El velo de la reina Mab" (1887) where the sculptor exalts Phidias, "rey ante un ejército de hermosuras que a tus ojos arrojan el magnífico *kitón* mostrando la esplendidez de la forma en sus cuerpos de rosa y de nieve" (*CC,* 52). Th. Gautier, using a more conservative spelling, speaks of a *chiton* in "A Charles Garnier." As we would expect, Leconte de Lisle is partial to the Greek *k* both in his original works and in his translations.

Kalofónica 'beautiful sounding' seems to have been compounded by Darío in opposition to the usual *cacofónico.* He uses two Greek words, *kalos* 'beautiful', *phone* 'sound' and the Latin suffix *-icus.*[19] In the semi-humorous setting of "Un ser-

---

[18] See Liddell and Scott, *Greek-English Lexicon,* Oxford, 1929, p. 1728.

[19] María Rosa Lida de Malkiel, *Juan de Mena,* México, 1950, p. 234 discusses a similar stylistic device peculiar to the Latinistic language of Mena and his group. They used such words as *çilénico* which actually are not borrowings from Latin, but analogous creations on the basis of Latin adjective suffixes. Cf. L. *hesperius, hespericus* and *dorius doricus.* For other examples in Darío, see *pánico* and *pandórica.*

món" (1892) we find this used to describe the "preacher's" words: "se remontaba kalofónica y extrahumana, hasta la cúpula" (*CC,* 279). The "preacher" is Castelar.

Thánatos is the Greek god of death that Darío evokes in two of his poems. Leconte de Lisle speaks of "Thanatos" in the *Iliade.* In Darío's morbid poem "Thánatos" Death is the "emperatriz y reina de la nada" (*OPC,* 747). Death is inevitable. In "Pax" (1915) Darío describes Death as smiling and happy because of the destruction caused by World War I. The reference to Krupp is to the huge munitions and steel plants of the Germans: "Krupp hace el crudo espanto que a Thánatos alegra" (*OPC,* 1063).

The word *Thanathopia,* the title of a morbid short story by Darío written in the manner of Poe, is problematic. This word has not been found in any of the authors Darío knew. There are, however, three possible explanations. First, Professor Cedric Hubbell Whitman has suggested that *thanathopia* was coined from the Greek word meaning 'a causing of death.' This explanation, in Darío's case, does not seem probable unless he was imitating this incorrect form from one of his models, who is unknown to us. A more direct source could be William Cullen Bryant's poem "Thanatopsis" 'view of death,' published in its entirety in his *Poems* (1822). Assuming that Darío was not imitating any French model, we are inclined to think that Bryant's poem is a reasonable explanation of *thanathopia,* which Darío probably did not coin himself. Finally it should be taken into consideration that Bryant's poem might have been translated into French with an erroneous transliteration of the title. If so, this most likely would have been Darío's source.

Kyrieleison 'Lord have mercy on us' is a Greek expression that Darío surely knew from the Mass. The fact that he writes it as one word is strong indication that he was influenced from having heard it. Then too, Flaubert repeatedly speaks of the "Kyrie eleïson" in Chapter iv of *La tentation de Saint Antoine* (1849). Moreover, in Verlaine's *Liturgies intimes* (1892) there is a poem with these Greek words as its title. In Darío's "Salmo" from *Baladas y canciones* (1896-1910) there is a confession of a mixture of "fuegos de pasión" and a longing for God, as we have seen on numerous other occasions in Darío:

> Del órgano el son
> me dé la oración
> y el *Kyrieleison.*
>
> Y la santa ciencia
> venga a mi conciencia
> por la penitencia. (*OPC, 956*)

The rhyme indicates that Darío put the stress on the last syllable, the meter, that he pronounced it in four syllables.

II *Words in -ida*

Of great interest, too, are words Darío uses that imitate the morphology of Greek patronymics. That is, he employs several words in *-ida* 'son of.' These words, ending in *-ide,* occur commonly in Leconte de Lisle and, to a lesser degree, in some of the other Parnassians. Flaubert, in *La tentation de Saint Antoine,* speaks of Hercules as *Amphytrionade.*[20] The Hermosilla translation of the *Iliad,* which Darío read, contains *Zeus Crónida.* The study of these forms in Darío's compositions shows that he used the French, not the Greek accent. There is but one exception: *homérida* 'son of Homer' or 'poet.' This is a term of eulogy in Darío that is also found in Anatole France's "La plume" (1891). In "Pórtico" (1896) Salvador Rueda is described as a "joven homérida." In Darío's essay "Leconte de Lisle" enthusiastic tribute is paid to this poet: "¡Homéricos funerales para quien fué homérida!" Leconte de Lisle's poetic genius makes him nothing less than the son of Homer.

Another of these words has the meaning of 'poet' in Darío. Darío boastfully points to himself as "yo, apolonida" in "Loor." There is certainly no modesty or uncertainty about

---

[20] Gustave Flaubert, *La tentation de Saint Antoine,* Paris, 1924, p. 152. The editor's correction is *Amphitryoniade.* Further quotations will be given in the text.

his status in literature, for Darío singles himself out as "the" poet. He is none other than the son of Apollo, a considerably more prestigious rank than that accorded to Leconte de Lisle. Darío probably imitated the form of Leconte de Lisle's *Apollonide* 'Ion.'

Panida 'son of Pan' in "Responso a Verlaine" describes this poet. However, the word is retracted, for it is not strong enough to describe Verlaine's sensuality. Verlaine is not the son of Pan; he is Pan himself, "Panida, Pan tú mismo" (*OPC*, 651). *Panida* retains its sensual connotation in "Revelación" (1907) and in "La vida y la muerte" from the *Lira póstuma*. In "Revelación" Darío, mysteriously animistic, looks toward a mountain in search of the "bicorne frente" that puts sun into "l'alma del panida." *Panida* occurs with a similar tone, synonymous with dionysian living, in "La vida y la muerte:"

> ¿Quién le da sangre al Panida?
> La Vida. (*OPC*, 978)

(See *bicorne* and *Pan*.)

Adanida 'son of Adam' describes the bear in "Canción de los osos" (1907): "vais en dos patas como el adanida" (*OPC*, 880). Marasso documents *abramides* and *ramide* in Saint Yves d'Alveydre's *Missión de l'Indeen Europe,* which Darío most likely did not read.

Ixionida 'son of Ixion' refers to the centaurs, excluding Chiron, and occurs in "El coloquio de los centauros" (1896). For example, Pholus emphasizes the sensuality of the centaurs by referring to their parents, Ixion and the cloud resembling Juno with whom Ixion was tricked into mating by Jupiter:

> El ixionida pasa veloz por la montaña,
> . . . .
> junto a la oculta fuente su mirada acaricia
> las curvas de las ninfas del séquito de Diana;
> pues en su cuerpo corre también la esencia humana,
> unida a la corriente de la savia divina
> y a la salvaje sangre que hay en la bestia equina. (*OPC*, 630)

III *Other "vocablos exóticos"*

The other "vocablos exóticos" that were so appealing to Darío, according to his aforementioned remark in his *Autobiografía,* are striking because of their poetic force in so many images. Mapes lists several of the names of Greek objects Darío uses; here we should like to fix our attention on some of his favorites to see how widely diffused they were in his French and Spanish models.

Ánfora (Corominas: *ánfora* first documented in Spanish in Andrés Laguna's *Pedazio Dioscorides Anazarbeo* (1555). This word evidently was not widely used in Spanish, for the documentation is scant. We find *ánfora* in Menéndez y Pelayo's "Epístola a Horacio" (1876). *Amphore* in Leconte de Lisle's "Thaliarque," "Lydé," "Glycère" and "Niobé" in *Poèmes antiques* as well as in Baudelaire's "Hymne à la Beauté," Mallarmé's sonnet "Ses purs ongles," Mendès's *Bacchus* and in selections by Laprade and Banville quoted below. This word is not as widely used as Marasso (p. 149) implies: "el vaso, la copa, se han convertido en el léxico parnasiano en ánfora." Nor is the meaning so limited.)

This container was widely used in Greece and Rome to hold wine, oil, honey and other liquids. In Leconte de Lisle's "Niobé" the amphora holds honey: "Le miel tombe en rayons des profondes amphores." Darío follows the primary ancient usage in that he customarily describes the *ánforas* as filled with wine. In "Bouquet" (1886) part of the history of the rose is that "En los banquetes de los antiguos griegos, esos pétalos se mezclaban en las ánforas con el vino" (*CC*, 219). In "Primaveral" Darío shows further fidelity to the ancient mode. First, his muse brings him "un ánfora griega" filled with wine, but also

> y una hermosa copa de oro,
> la base henchida de perlas,
> para que bebiese el vino. (*OPC,* 572)

We see that Darío regards the amphora solely as a storage vessel, not a cup. Whether the Parnassians used this word to mean any cup, as Marasso believes, is a question. Let us see. In Laprade's "La coupe" the amphora is certainly not a cup:

> Le vin, c'est sa lumière et sa chaleur; l'amphore
> Cache en ses flancs obscurs des gouttes de soleil.
>
> Toi, par qui, d'une lèvre où le rire étincelle,
> La chanson radieuse à plus grands flots ruisselle;
> Toi, dont ma coupe pleine atteste le pouvoir,
> Je t'ai vu, le carquois sonnant sur tes épaules,
> Descendre, ô dieu joyeux, sur nos coteaux des Gaules,
> Et tes cheveux flotter, et les rubis pleuvoir!

At one moment Banville's poetic utilization of this word is more imaginative than either Darío's or Laprade's. In "Au laurier de la turbie" in *Les exilés* he speaks of "...les flots que la mer jette de ses amphores." In Banville's "Le festin des dieux" there is an insistence upon the amphora as a storage vessel for wine that is very similar to Darío's usage in "Primaveral:"

> Le vin dormait, vermeil, dans les amphores d'or,
> D'où, par milliers, courant en leur agile essor,
> Des nymphes aux beaux bras, formant de riants groupes,
> Avec des cris charmants le versaient dans les coupes.

There is no doubt about it. The Parnassians' gods are no less decorous than Darío's. At times, both seem to prefer to drink from cups, not amphorae. By no means do the Parnassians use this word to designate any cup.

In view of the limited documentation of this word in Spanish, Darío probably learned it from the Parnassians. Yet, this does not prevent him at times from using the word in a completely "castizo" setting. There is a "castizo"-Parnassian duality in the very Spanish "Otro dezir." The form is Spanish, but the poetic utilization of the word is similar to that sometimes found in the Parnassians. The invitation is extended to "Del ánfora en que está el viejo / vino anacreóntico, bebe" (*OPC*, 666). This duality appears again in the equally Spanish "Elogio de la seguidilla." The amphora is used metaphorically to describe this poetic form that Darío actually employs in this poem: "Pequeña ánfora lírica de vino llena, / compuesto por la dulce musa Alegría" (*OPC*, 644).

Darío's other point of reference to the *ánfora* is that of its graceful shape. In general, this vase was a tall container tapering to a point at the bottom, with a slender-necked top. Two handles, extending from the mouth to the body, were the distinguishing characteristics. In the "Coloquio de los centauros" Venus is complimented thus: "Tiene las formas puras del ánfora, . . ." The swan's neck is twice likened to the shape of the amphora. In "Acuarela" (1887) the swan is described as "enarcando el cuello en la forma del brazo de una lira o del ansa de una ánfora" (*CC*, 41). Again in "Blasón" (1896) the swan's neck is pictured in terms of the *ánfora*: "De la forma de un brazo de lira/ y del asa de un ánfora griega" (*OPC*, 612).

Clámide (Corominas: *clámide* is first documented in Balmes, 1848. Documentation of this word is limited in Spanish; we find it in Menéndez y Pelayo's "Epístola a Horacio." Among Darío's French models, in Laprade's "Éleusis," Flaubert's *La tentation de Saint Antoine* and in Leconte de Lisle.)

In Leconte de Lisle's "Le reveil d'Hélios" (1852), *khlamyde* contributes to a brilliant image: "Le jeune homme divin, nourrisson de Délos,/Dans sa khlamyde d'or quitte l'azur des flots." The same image recurs in his "Dies irae" to describe the dawn. However, Laprade had earlier described Apollo wearing a "chlamyde d'or" in "Éleusis" (1844). The word *clámide* in Darío has been commonly attributed to his readings of Leconte de Lisle. Darío uses the more conservative form *clámide* in "Mater pulchra." The poem, dedicated to General J. Santos Zelaya on the death of his mother, re-creates a plastic scene of ancient times with the salient figure of Julius Caesar mourning his mother's death:

> Es Grecia, es Roma. Clámides
> y togas. Es el tiempo maravilloso. Es
> el Partenón, el templo de Apolo, las Pirámides,
> las glorias hechas ruinas que volverán después. (*OPC*, 999)

63

Bárbitos is a Greek word used as such by Darío. It is not in any edition of the *DRAE*. Littré gives the French form as *barbiton*. We have not found this word in any of Darío's models. There are two possible conclusions. First, if it does exist among them, it is only in very isolated cases. Second, Darío was most likely struck by this word in Baráibar's translation of Anacreon, published by the "Biblioteca Clásica" in 1884.

In "El sátiro sordo" (1888) the *barbitos* is but one of a whole register of musical instruments in a description of Orpheus' song. This word was first used by Anacreon for the lyre itself. Horace, in his *Odes* III, 26, speaks of this instrument. In "El sátiro sordo" Darío tells of the verse "que acompaña el bárbitos en la oda" (*CC*, 113). This line seems best explained by the fact that in Anacreon's first ode, commented on by Baráibar, *bárbitos* is given the meaning of *lyre*.

Cítara (Corominas: *cítara* is first documented in 1499 in H. Núñez de Toledo. The derivative *citarista* appears in Góngora in 1591.[21] However, Dámaso Alonso, *La lengua*, p.52 says *cítara* is one of a group of learned words in Spanish dating back to the thirteenth century. He further states that *cítara* was common among the Spanish Latinistic poets from the end of the fourteenth to the beginning of the sixteenth centuries, especially in Fray Iñigo de Mendoza, Pérez de Guzmán, Hernán Mexía and Álvarez Gato: *cítara* in Góngora in 1602, according to Alonso. *Autoridades*: in Lope's *Dorotea* (1632): "Como llamar al Ruiseñor cíthara de pluma; que por la misma razón se havía de llamar la cíthara Ruiseñor de palo."[22] We also find this word in Leandro Fernández de Moratín, Quintana, Bello, Valera, Menéndez y Pelayo and, among Darío's French models,

[21] Besides this learned form *cítara*, Corominas says that there are three other variants in Spanish. (1) V. L. *citera*, documented in *Appendix Probi* No. 23 > O.Sp. *cedra*, found in Berceo's *Duelo*. (2) With a semi-learned character, L. *cithara* > *cítola*, also in Berceo, as well as Juan Ruiz and as late as Juan de Mena. (3) *Guitarra* < Ar. *kitâra* and this < Gr. *kithara*.

[22] Cf. in Góngora's *Soledad primera* the metaphor "cítharas de pluma" and in Darío's "Epitalamio bárbaro" the similar "flautas de pluma."

in Banville, Leconte de Lisle, who uses the form *kithare,* and in Rimbaud's "Antique I."[23])

In the Banvillesque atmosphere of "Canción de carnaval" (1896) Darío exhorts his muse, "Sé lírica y sé bizarra;/ con la cítara sé griega." Within the image itself, *cítara* is part of the gaiety and animation Darío has created. The image as a whole complements the atmosphere of this song of childlike enthusiasm.

Banville's "La cithare" in *Les exilés* emerges as important because of the description of the potent effects on nature of Orpheus' song:

> Son Ode avait donné la vie aux noirs déserts,
> Car les arbres lointains, entraînés par la force
> Des vers, orme touffu, chêne à la rude écorce,
> Étaient venus, cédant au charme de la voix;
> Et voici qu'à présent le feuillage d'un bois
> Mélodieux, immense et rempli de murmures,
> Sur le front du chanteur étendait ses ramures;
> Les rocs avaient fendu la terre en un moment:
>
> . . . .
>
> Du fond de l'éther vaste et des cieux inconnus
> Les oiseaux, déployant leur vol, étaient venus;
> Puis, gravissant les monts neigeux, mornes colosses,
> Les animaux tremblants et les bêtes féroces
> Et les lions étaient venus. Dans le ravin,
> Ils écoutaient, léchant les pieds du Roi divin,
> Ou pensifs, accroupis dans une vague extase.

Similar supernatural effects on nature are pictured in the amusingly fantastic atmosphere of "El sátiro sordo" (1888). Compare, for example, these lines: "Las palmeras derramaban su polen, las semillas reventaban, los leones movían blandamen-

---

[23] [Charles Marie René] Leconte de Lisle, *Poésies complètes,* Paris, 1858, p. 80. Moratín is quoted in Federico Ruiz Morcuende, *Vocabulario de D. Leandro Fernández de Moratín,* I, 319. Manuel José Quintana, *Poesías,* Madrid, 1927, pp. 88, 207. Andrés Bello, *Colección de poesías originales,* Paris, 1870, p. 177. Juan Valera, *Romances y poemas,* Madrid, 1885, pp. 272, 284. Marcelino Menéndez y Pelayo, *Edición nacional de las obras completas,* Santander, 1949-1955, LXI, 158. All future quotations from these works will be given in the text. DRAE, as the reader undoubtedly realizes, signifies *Diccionario de la Real Academia Española.*

te su crin. Una vez voló un clavel de su tallo hecho mariposa roja, y una estrella descendió fascinada y se tornó flor de lis." Further on this idea is reiterated: "Los enormes troncos se conmovieron, y hubo rosas que se deshojaron y lirios que se inclinaron lánguidamente como en un dulce desmayo. Porque Orfeo hacía gemir los leones y llorar los guijarros con la música de su lira rítmica." Although Darío acknowledged his debt to Mendès, Flaubert and, of course, Hugo, Banville must certainly be taken into account.

The over-all atmosphere of "El sátiro sordo" has been termed Lucianesque by Marasso and later critics: "La ironía, la gracia, hasta el lirismo que se amplifica con el 'vaste souffle' de Hugo son lucianescos" (Marasso, p. 351). Marasso assumes that Darío might have known French translations of Lucian since, according to Marasso, Baráibar's version of Lucian was not published until 1889, a year after *Azul* . . . . Yet, in Mejía Sánchez's invaluable article we learn that the *Obras completas* of Lucian were among those volumes published by the "Biblioteca Clásica" prior to Darío's trip to Chile in 1886. However, what we actually see is that this is one of the many instances in which Darío's sources are so well assimilated that it is difficult to be sure of his exact model. The prevailing tone, then, is Lucianesque and Banvillesque.

In Leconte de Lisle's "Médailles antiques" the *kithare* is simply an accompaniment to the dance:

> Les cheveux noués d'un lien de fleurs,
> Une Ionienne aux belles couleurs
> Danse sur la mousse, au son des kithares.

Siringa (*Siringa* is first documented in Nebrija according to Corominas, who also finds *siringa* in Juan de Valdés and *xeringa* 'jeringa' in Quevedo. *Siringa,* as a musical instrument, does not appear in the *DRAE* until 1925. Francisco Nieto Molina wrote *Fábula de Pan y Siringa* (1764). In Valera's translation *Dafnis y Cloe* we find, "Siringa, . . . no era flauta pastoril en lo antiguo, sino virgen hermosa, con buena voz y arte en el canto." Littré: in Chénier. We also have found *syrinx* in

Laprade, Leconte de Lisle, Mallarmé and in Flaubert's *La tentation de Saint Antoine* [*p.* 147].[24])

Siringa is a poetic word for rustic flute and takes its name from Syrinx, the Arcadian nymph who was transformed into a reed to escape lustful Pan.[25] Normally, as in Darío, Pan, the fauns and the satyrs are depicted with a seven tube flute, with an attendant note of sensuality:

> En la pasional siringa
> brotaron las siete voces
> que en siete carrizos puso
> Pan.   (*OPC,* 715)

In "Por el influjo de la primavera" (1905) the erotic element is plainly stated in the adjective *pasional*. In "A Rubencito" this same connotation is strongly implied in Darío's advice to his son, "no oigas a la faunesa que te lanza su grito,/ ni al fauno extraordinario que su siringa suene." (See *faunesa*.)

Pan and the members of his cortege are most commonly associated with the *siringa*: "Pan trae el ritmo con la egregia siringa" (*OPC,* 692). The same is quite true with the Parnassians and some of the earlier advocates of *l'art pour l'art*. In Laprade's "Éleusis:"

> Pan, le riche berger, surveille ses domaines.
> Les Nymphes près de lui sont assises en rond;
> Deux rameaux verdoyants jaillissent de son front;
> Sa main tient le syrinx appliqué sur sa lèvre,
> Et le gazon en fleurs couvre ses pieds de chèvre.

Further on Laprade properly defines this instrument as "le syrinx des Faunes." In "L'après-midi d'un faune" Mallarmé refers to its origin: "Tâche donc, instrument des fuites, ô maligne/Syrinx, de refleurir aux lacs où tu m'attends!" In

[24] Victor de Laprade, *Oeuvres poétiques,* Paris, [1878-1881?], I, 155, 165. Stéphane Mallarmé, *Poésies,* Paris, 1949, p. 528. All future quotations from these works will be given in the text.

[25] In Virgil's *Eclogues,* II, 32-33: "Pan primum calamos cera coniungere plures / instituit." Tradition first presented the *siringa* as an instrument of the Arcadian shepherds. Among the ancients it was an emblem of pastoral life. The Latin poets also presented the shepherd playing this instrument, but not with its primitive name. Denominations for it vary even in the same author.

Leconte de Lisle's "Klytie" it is simply referred to as "la molle syrinx" and in "Les plaintes du cyclope" it is "la claire syrinx."

However, in "El sátiro sordo" a variation is introduced, for it is not Pan, but Orpheus who is identified with the syrinx. Orpheus, with his songs of Jove, Eros, Aphrodite, Bacchus with his cortege and "las intimidades del aire y de la tierra" explains "las notas armónicas que brotan de una siringa" (*CC,* 113). In "Responso a Verlaine" (1896) the *siringa,* here conceived of as a pastoral instrument, in contrast with the lofty Olympic lyre, receives the magic touch of Verlaine:

> Padre y maestro mágico, liróforo celeste
> que al instrumento olímpico y a la siringa agreste
> diste tu acento encantador;   (*OPC,* 651)

The pagan *siringa* figures in "Palimpsesto II" (1908) in such a way that we see an example of what will be discussed in detail in subsequent chapters: a leveling of Christian and pagan figures, whereby Rome comes to signify both. "He aquí que la siringa, la flauta pagana, crecerá y aparecerá más tarde en los tubos de los órganos de las basílicas, por premio al sátiro que buscó a Dios" (*CC,* 290).

(Also see *ninfa, sátiro* and *centauro.*)

Tímpano (The *tímpano* 'kettledrum' is included in Covarrubias' *Tesoro de la lengua castellana* (1611). *Autoridades*: in Villegas' *Eróticas* (1618), "Detén, pues, los crueles/Tympanos de la cándida Cybeles." This word also appears in Edmond Saglio's *Dictionnaire* and in *Hymnes orphiques,* XXVI, translation of Leconte de Lisle. *Tympan* is also found in A. Ferdinand Hérold's *Au hasard des chemins*[26] and is common in Flaubert's *La tentation de Saint Antoine* [pp. 137, 155, 164 and 483].)

In a previously quoted passage from "El sátiro sordo" the *tímpano* is one of the instruments in the musical catalogue Darío makes: "Así explicó la melodía de una arpa eolia, el susurro de una arboleda, el ruido ronco de un caracol y las notas armónicas que brotan de una siringa. Cantó del verso,

---

[26] A. Ferdinand Hérold, *Au hasard des chemins,* Paris, 1900, p. 30.

que baja del cielo y place a los dioses, del que acompaña el bárbitos en la oda y el tímpano en el peán" (*CC*, 113). This instrument contributes to an entirely different effect in the sarcastic liturgical-like chant of "Canción del oro" (1888): "Cantemos el oro, ... sonante como un coro de tímpanos" (*CC*, 73).

Atlántico (*Autoridades*: *atlantes* are statues of men placed to support architraves, and because of the way in which they are arranged, the architecture is described as *orden atlántico*. The word *atlante* was introduced with reference to the myth of the titan Atlas. The ancients believed he supported the heavens on his shoulders by the great knowledge he had of the course of the sun, the moon and the stars.)

In Darío's "La ninfa" the garden, which recalls the one in Chapter x of Villiers de l'Isle-Adam's *Isis,* is filled with ancient statues. The garden is populated by bronze "discóbolos," muscular "gladiadores" and "vigorosos telamones del orden atlántico." The *telamones* are synonymous for *atlantes.* Darío, who prefers the word *telamón,* uses it in such a way in "La ninfa" that it seems he must have corroborated his information in a dictionary or manual. Like many of the other images with architectural terms, this one is neither graceful nor effective. It seems rather to be a display of erudition. Similarly, the *telamones* figure in the group of statues in the workshop in "Arte y hielo." It is an enumeration heavy with technical terms: "Ved aquí estatuas, medallas, metopas, cariátides, grifos y telamones" (*CC*, 109).

Metopa (Corominas: *Métopa*<L. *metopa*; *metopa* is first documented in B. de Balbuena (1624). Corominas says, "La posición dentro del verso en este poeta indica que acentuaba metópa como la hace gráficamente *Aut.*" The Academy adopted the Latin accent. *Métopes* in Gautier's "Ce que disent les hirondelles," in Laprade's *Questions d'art et de morale* and commonly in André Lefèvre's chapter on Greek art in *Les merveilles de l'architecture.*)

The metopae are also part of the weighty list of figures in "Arte y hielo." *Metopa* is again used in "J. J. Palma" in

Azul . . . . In this tribute to Palma, Darío uses *metopa* figuratively, "Ya de un corintio templo cincela una metopa..." (*OPC*, 594). For Laprade, however, the metopae are perhaps as alluring as the amphora is to Darío. The metopae connote a great beauty and harmony that is characteristic, to Laprade, of the ancient Greek culture he admires so:

> Étudiez au contraire le temps grec: quelle ordonnance harmonieuse, quelle exactitude dans les proportions, que de grâce et de sévérité à la fois dans ces lignes calmes et reposées;
>
> . . . .
>
> Voyez, sur l'acropole d'Athènes, s'élever les colonnes du Parthénon comme de belles vierges rangées en ordre à la procession des Panathénées; elles portent leurs gracieux chapiteaux comme des corbeilles de fleurs. Dans cette lumière étincelante et pure du ciel de l'Attique, les angles des frontons se découpent nettement, tous les détails des métopes et des frises restent dans leur élévation à portée de l'oeil humain, et les immortelles sculptures de Phidias se déroulent devant vous. L'imagination ne saurait rien ajouter à cet ensemble qui n'en rompît l'harmonie; la raison la plus géométrique et la plus sévère n'y saurait rien retrancher; vous le sentez, et vous avez l'idée de la perfection; cela est complet en soi comme l'existence d'un Dieu.

Cariátide (Corominas: *cariátide* is first documented in Sigüenza, 1605. Littré: in Chateaubriand. Banville wrote *Les cariatides* (1842). *Cariatides* is part of the subtitle to Sully Prudhomme's "La nature et la tradition" (1878); also in Lefèvre's chapter on Greek art in *Les merveilles de l'architecture*.)

The caryatids, like the *telamones* and *metopas,* are in the ponderous, scientific enumeration of statues in the sculptor's workshop in "Arte y hielo." However, there is a marked variance between the usual idea of the caryatids and Darío's presentation of them in "La ninfa." They are customarily women clothed in flowing robes, used in place of columns, as are the *telamones* or *atlantes*. In art the caryatids normally show a tranquil attitude that contrasts with the violent attitude of the *telamones*. However, in "La ninfa" they are "cariátides todas blancas y lascivas." Darío ascribes a strongly sensual note to them.

Canéfora (Corominas: first documented in Spanish in Clairac and Sáenz, *Diccionario de arquitectura e ingeniería,* Madrid, 1887. However, we are predating this word, which has been located in Menéndez y Pelayo's "La hechicera" (1875). *Canéfora* also occurs in Gutiérrez Nájera. Littré: in Chateaubriand and Hugo, *Odes,* IV, 10; also in Leconte de Lisle's "Niobé.")

In "Friso" (1896) homage is paid to the beauty and grace of Eunice by comparing her to the canephorae, young Greek girls chosen for their nobility and beauty to carry baskets of offerings on their heads to the temples as part of the sacred ceremonies:

> No más gallarda se encamina al templo
> Canéfora gentil, ni más riente
> llega la musa a quien favor prodiga
> el divino Sminteo, que mi amada
> al tender hacia mí sus tersos brazos. (*OPC,* 654)

In Leconte de Lisle's "Niobé" the "Kanephores" serve fruit to the royal guests. In Darío's "Responso a Verlaine" (1896) the canephorae are among the pagan figures that Darío hopes will give Verlaine due homage: "Que púberes canéforas te ofrenden el acanto" (*OPC,* 652). The graceful air about them as they walked to the temples offered a beautiful subject to art that has been reproduced in sculpture and on painted vases. In "Toašt" (1896) Darío salutes some of the world's famed art treasures:

> Y el pórtico del templo que habita el Numen sacro,
> el altar donde se alce su augusto simulacro,
> y en teoría suave canéforas hermosas. (*OPC,* 968)

This reference might be to the figures carved by Phidias on the frieze of the cella of the Parthenon; they are commonly believed to be canephorae. The delight Darío seems to feel in evoking the canephorae is similar, but not early as intense, to that seen in Laprade's previously quoted eulogy of the Parthenon: "les immortelles sculptures de Phidias."

It seems, then, that of all the Parnassians and pre-Parnassians such as Laprade, Leconte de Lisle is a particularly important influence in explaining Darío's transliterations. Leconte de Lisle's orthography had Darío's full approval because of its aristocratic effect on the printed page. Darío's own experimentation with such spelling was just one aspect of his far-reaching curiosity towards matters that would contribute to freshness of expression and to the creation of an art for the elite. Darío was, however, relatively conservative in his utilization of these transliterations, for they are not particularly common in his works. His admiration fortunately does not lead him to a slavish and wholesale imitation, but rather to a discreet selection in accordance with his artistic temperament and tastes. Although Darío's knowledge of Spanish literature certainly included an awareness of the struggle in Spanish between etymological and phonetic spelling, his transliterations were stimulated largely by his enthusiasm for this device in Leconte de Lisle. This explanation is the most reasonable, notwithstanding the fact that the tradition of erudite orthography was revived in the nineteenth century by Menéndez y Pelayo. By no means do we exclude Menéndez y Pelayo's influence; it is simply a matter of establishing degrees of importance.

Darío's transliterations show that he knew even less Greek than Latin as he himself implied in his remark on the value of his Jesuit education. His erroneously accented *anagké* is testimony to this. Although some might contend that this very argument is an indication that Darío might have coined *Thanathopia,* we could not agree. Darío was too aware of his own limitations in Greek to be so venturesome. Certainly his successful coinage of *kalofónica* and like morphological forms did not require much daring since he had somewhat of a precedent in Spanish in the analogous creations of Juan de Mena and his group. (See note 19.) Here, as elsewhere, Darío proceeds with discretion and good judgment. His words in *-ida* are almost exclusively a French influence; with the exception of *homérida* Darío follows the French accent on these words. Hermosilla's translation of the *Iliad,* with such forms as *Zeus Crónida,* was a more limited influence.

As for the other "vocablos exóticos" that Darío describes

as part of the "mina que explotar" that he found in his modern French readings, the documentation shows that these words are, for the most part, found in both the Spanish and French authors known to Darío. Admittedly his remarks give more stress to his French readings. Yet we do not consider this surprising; such an emphasis is perfectly understandable and almost to be expected since his French readings did have the charm of being relatively new to him. We should not expect him to give the same stress to his Spanish readings, which had for so long been a part of him. In general, the "castizo" element in Darío's Greco-Roman vocabulary has too long been subordinated to the Parnassian influence. He had an immense background of readings, both French and Spanish. The result had to be an intermingling of influences. Indeed, mulling over these words in his French models provided the stimulus for incorporating them into his active poetic vocabulary. It is, however, unjust and inaccurate to say simply that this language is a Parnassian influence.[27]

Darío often surpasses his models in his utilization of these words. The Parnassians and such others as Gautier and Laprade normally use them in a straightforward and traditional manner. Darío, however, is enthralled with the marvelous evocative power of these substantives and extracts as much as possible from them. Venus' graceful body is compared to the "formas puras" of the amphora. The swan's neck is described in terms of the ". . . asa de un ánfora griega." With a poet as accomplished as Darío such words can and do acquire intimate poetic meaning. He is sensitive to nuances; one of these words arouses many emotions. *Siringa* strongly suggests sensuality in "Por el influjo de la primavera" and in "A Rubencito." In "Palimpsesto II" the same word acquires a profoundly religious connotation. At times Darío is able to re-create an historical era or give a touch of local color with these words. Consider

[27] Arturo Torres-Rioseco in *Casticismo y americanismo en la obra de Rubén Darío,* Cambridge, 1931, says that Mapes, because of an insufficient knowledge of Spanish literature, attributed certain aspects of Darío's versification to his French readings. Indeed, Mapes in general does not pay adequate attention to the Spanish tradition.

clámide in "Mater pulchra" and *siringa* and *tímpano* in "El sátiro sordo." The architectural terms tend to generate a pseudo-erudite air as seen in "Arte y hielo." There are a few exceptions. In "La ninfa" the *cariátides* convey intense sensuality; in "Friso" and "Toast," beauty.

Beauty and sensuality are, in fact, significant reasons for Darío's attraction to this vocabulary. He admires the beauty of the remote Greco-Roman world whether it be represented in the suggested sound of a *tímpano* or *cítara* or in the contours of the *ánfora*. In the following chapters on the divinities we shall see how potent the beauty and sensuality of the Greco-Roman civilization were. The underlying truth in explaining this lexicon is that Darío was bent upon creating an art for the elite; such words could appeal only to the "iniciados." So it was that Latin words and quotations, Greek transliterations and assorted other "vocablos exóticos" brought to the fore a wealth of material for the revitalization of Spanish poetry. With zest, but above all with talent, Darío uses this lexicon to create compositions ranging from the height of frivolity to the depths of mystery.

CHAPTER IV

THE ROLE OF THE LESSER DIVINITIES

The many images Darío constructs around the lesser divinities will show even more vividly to what extent he was captivated by the beauty and sensuality of the Greco-Roman world. We also shall see illustrated what is meant by the term "Grecia afrancesada," normally used to characterize Darío's mythological re-creations. He was charmed by Greece and Rome as seen through eighteenth-century France. He relived that era along with a whole generation of French writers. The "fêtes galantes" that Darío delights in are customarily credited primarily to Verlaine's book of the same name, published in 1869. In reality, these elements are found prior to that in Gautier and Gérard de Nerval, in Hugo's "La fête chez Thérèse" and in certain poems by Laprade and, above all, Banville. Many poets that Darío knew were enchanted with the elegant statues of mythological personages that adorned the formal gardens at Versailles. These marble figures are like the "divins fossiles" to which Sully Prudhomme pays tribute in "Les Vénus" from *Stances* (1865).

The byword of that admired period was "volupté." Edmond and Jules de Goncourt aptly epitomize the spirit of the times in *L'amour au dix-huitième siècle* (1875):

> La Volupté, cette volupté universelle, qui se dégage des choses vivantes comme des choses inanimées, qui se mêle à la parole, qui frémit dans le livre, qui palpite dans la musique, qui est la voix, l'accent, la forme de ce monde, la femme la retrouve dans l'art du temps plus matérielle et pour ainsi dire incarnée. La statue, le tableau, sollicitent son regard par un agrément irritant, par la grâce amusante et piquante du joli. Sous le ciseau du sculpteur, sous le pinceau du peintre, dans une nuée

d'Amours, tout un Olympe naît du marbre, sort de la toile, qui n'a d'autre divinité que la coquetterie.[1]

The reigning ideal, then, was "le libertinage des passions méchantes, la Luxure du Mal!" (p. 120). Woman was thoughtfully absolved from obedience to traditional attitudes: "Modestie, bienséance, le dix-huitième siècle travaille à dispenser la femme de ces misères" (p. 61).

Exactly how much of this permissiveness is reflected in Darío's writings remains to be seen. For the most part, though, the over-all atmosphere of eighteenth-century France in Darío is a French influence. The documentation, however, will tell whether the lexicon involved can categorically be labelled a Parnassian influence. Since ultimately we shall show a transformation in Darío's mythology towards 1897, it is essential to note the chronology of the works discussed. The dates of the poems usually correspond to the collection in which they appeared.

I Fabulous Creatures

Egipán (*DRAE,* 1956: 'ser fabuloso, mitad cabra, mitad hombre.' First appears in 1936 ed. of *DRAE.* Hugo: "Les aegipans étant fameux comme les vins" and "l'aegipan de Crète."[2] In Hugo's "Le satyre": "Le paon de sa queue insulta l'aegipan." From Leconte de Lisle's *Poèmes antiques,* "l'Aigipan lascif" in "La source," "L'Aigipan moqueur" in "Thyoné" and "l'Aigipan" plays a flute in "Paysage." Note the literal spelling. *Aegipan* in Gautier's "Bûchers et tombeaux" and commonly in Mendès' *Bacchus.*)

Darío's "Por el influjo de la primavera" (1905) describes the effect of this season, associated with the amorous, by the use of Greek, Latin, Florentine and Parisian suggestions. An-

---

[1] Edmond and Jules de Goncourt, *L'amour au dix-huitième siècle,* Paris, 1875, p. 13. Future quotations from this source will be given in the text. Two other works of theirs were also read by Darío and his French models: *La femme au dix-huitième siècle* (1867) and *L'art au dix-huitième siècle* (1873).

[2] Victor Hugo, *La légende des siècles,* ed. Jacques Truchet, Paris, 1950, p. 411. Future quotations from this work will be given in the text.

cient pagan rites and dead desires are reborn in an image charged with sensuality, lent by the coupling of this horned satyr and the bacchante:

> Imaginaos un roble
> que diera una rosa fresca;
> un buen egipán latino
> con una bacante griega
> y parisiense . . .   (*OPC*, 715)

In "Bûchers et tombeaux" Gautier links these two creatures in such a way that a startling contrast is achieved; they are the symbol of life, love and sensuality in the presence of death:

> Entre les fleurs et les acanthes,
> Dans le marbre joyeusement,
> Amours, aegipans et bacchantes
> Dansaient autour du monument;

The *egipán* figures as an even more erotic creature in "Madrigal exaltado" (1905):

> El bosque se encuentra estrecho
> al egipán en acecho
> cuando respira ese pecho.   (*OPC*, 733)

In the strange poem "A un pintor" (1907), which discovers the sensual and aspires to the spiritual, Darío suddenly leaves his fearful vision of death to return to seek color in rather Ovidian-like forests, populated with sylvan deities:

> Vamos a cazar colores,
> ilusión los bosques dan,
> las driadas brillan flores
> y alegría el egipán.   (*OPC*, 807)

In this plastic image the *egipán* appears as a merrymaking creature, distinct from his previous sensual portrayals.

    Sileno (*Autoridades*: in Saavedra Fajardo's *República literaria* (1648): "En los Montes Sátyros, Panes, Silenos, Silvanos, Orcades y Centauros."[3] *Silène* in Ferdinand Hérold's "Le cor-

---

[3] Gayley, in *The Classic Myths*, sums up the lesser divinities of the earth. See especially pp. 45-46, 186 and 191.

tège de Dionysos," Leconte de Lisle's "Kybèle," in Mendès's *Bacchus* and in Sully Prudhomme's *Stances* there is the poem "Silène.")

Among the numerous satyrs or sileni, creatures half man and half goat, one was outstanding, Silenus. He had been the guardian and tutor of young Bacchus and, in later years, he was the constant companion of the god of wine. Such is the portrayal in Darío's "Respecto a Horacio" (1893). The scene Darío describes is from an amphora: "bajo la viña el gran Baco en su florida juventud . . . cerca está la figura de Sileno, que ríe viendo danzar un coro de faunos" (*CC,* 221). Silenus also appears as one fond of dancing in "El sátiro sordo" (1888) where the deaf satyr, "el rey caprípede bailaba delante de sus faunos, beodo y haciendo gestos como Sileno" (*CC,* 113). Thus far, Darío dwells upon the most traditional aspect of Silenus as the jovial attendant of Bacchus. The joviality that Darío describes, however, is due in large measure to the gladness that comes of wine, a truth that Sully Prudhomme makes quite apparent in "Silène." Here we see Silenus in his usual state of intoxication, leaning on his donkey for support:

> Silène boit. Sa tête est molle sur son cou;
> Dédaigneux d'un soutien, il s'incline et se cambre,
> Tend sa coupe en tremblant, lui parle, y goûte l'ambre,
> Et vante sa sagesse avec un oeil de fou.
>
> Il laisse au gré de l'âne osciller son enflure;
> L'essaim des nymphes rit sur le rideau des cieux;
> Tendre, et les doigts errants dans une chevelure,
> Il rend grâce à Bacchus, qui rajeunit les vieux.

In "Arte y hielo" (1888) a silenus apears as a statue in a manner reminiscent of eighteenth-century France as did Silenus above. However, this statue speaks: "Pero un sileno calmó al artista hablándole con sus labios de mármol desde su pedestal" (*CC,* 110).

Sátiro (Corominas: Sátiro, first documented in Nebrija, appears in *Don Quijote* I, 25 and many other classics according to Corominas. Dámaso Alonso, *La lengua . . .,* p. 71: *sátiro* is one of the words common in the Spanish Latinistic poets from

the end of the fourteenth century to the beginning of the sixteenth century; p. 63 indicates its occurrence in Santillana. First
appeared in Góngora in 1594. *Autoridades*: in Lope's *Dorotea*
(1632), "Amor a Venus cándida, / Porque en los brazos
hórridos / La vió de un feo Sátyro, / Lloró con tiernas lágry-
mas." Later documented in Nicolás Fernández de Moratín
(*DE*), Leandro Fernández de Moratín (*Voc.*), Quintana
(*Poesías*, p. 166), Valera (*Obras*, XII, 46, 62, 119), Menéndez y Pelayo (*Obras*, LXI, 113) and in Gutiérrez Nájera. In
Hugo (*La légende*, p. 411), Musset and Heredia.[4] Also in
Laprade's "Les deux muses," Leconte de Lisle's "Khirôn,"
throughout Flaubert's *La tentation de Saint Antoine*, in Banville's "Le triomphe de Bacchos" and "La cithare," in Sully
Prudhomme's "La néréide" and in Mendès's *Bacchus*.)

In Darío, the satyr plays many roles. In "Retrato de
Watteau" (1887) the Santiago lady, who seems to be Parisian
until the very end, is giving the final touch to her toilette. Hers
is an elaborate boudoir filled with replicas of the satyrs, sirens,
dolphins and tritons so much in vogue in eighteenth-century
France. The satyr here appears as one of those decorative
elements: "y le ríe con audacia un sátiro de bronce que sostiene
entre los pámpanos de su cabeza un candelabro" (*CC*, 47).
The satyr appears similarly, as an adornment, in "Arte y hielo"
(1888), but with the marked lasciviousness often associated
with satyrs: "¿Venís en busca de adornos para vuestros jardines? Contemplad ese sátiro con su descarada risa lasciva y
sus pezuñas de cabra" (*CC*, 109). The satyr in both stories
comes from the elegant and voluptuous eighteenth-century
France: "Para vosotras, mujeres queridas, haré sátiros y sirenas,
que serán la joya de vuestros tocadores" (*CC*, 108). In "La
ninfa" (1888), a Parisian story in the manner of Mendès,
Silvestre and Maizeroy, this same air of the France described
by the Goncourt brothers persists, with the culmination of the
sensual connotation of the satyr in the words of the diabolic

---

[4] Alfred de Musset, *Poésies et comédies*, Lyon, 1946, p. 64. José-Maria de
Heredia, *Poésies complètes*, Paris, 1924, p. 37. Future quotations from these
works will be given in the text.

Lesbia: "¡Bah! Para mí los sátiros. Y quisiera dar vida a mis bronces, y si esto fuese posible, mi amante sería uno de esos velludos semidioses" (*CC*, 61).

The reputation of the satyrs is such that as a rule their sensuality is implicit in the descriptions painted by the various French authors mentioned above. Apart from that, they seem to acknowledge these beings as just another part of the whole dionysiac retinue. They do not accord the satyrs the detailed attention that Darío gives them. In Laprade's "Les deux muses" the satyr appears in a traditional manner. He is a frolicsome woodland creature who loves to play his flute and dance:

> J'ai vu mes gais chevreaux et mes brebis paisibles
> Souvent bondir au son de pipeaux invisibles;
> Puis, un Satyre, au loin, apparaissait dansant.

In Banville's "Le triomphe de Bacchos" the satyrs are clearly members of Bacchus' cortege:

> Le tigre indien, le lynx, les panthères tachées,
> Suivent devant lui, par des guirlandes attachées,
> Les chèvres des monts, que, réjouis par de doux vins,
> Mènent en dansant les Satyres et les Sylvains.

In Banville's "La cithare" they are simply "Satyres champêtres." In Leconte de Lisle's "Khirôn" the satyrs are busy at what they enjoy the most: "Les Satyres guetteurs des Nymphes au sein nu."

Darío, on the other hand, is very knowledgeable concerning the satyr. Their possible real existence is a point at issue in "La ninfa." The "sabio" interrupts Lesbia to document the actual existence of various mythological beings: ". . . Los sátiros y los faunos, los hipocentauros y las sirenas, han existido, como las salamandras y el ave Fénix" (*CC,* 61). He adds that San Antonio Abad, in search of the hermit Pablo, met not only a centaur, but also a satyr, and "la última parte de su contrahecho cuerpo remataba con pies de cabra." Moreover, "Afirma San Jerónimo, que en tiempo de Constantino Magno se condujo a Alejandría un sátiro vivo."[5] Also, "Dice Alberto Magno que en su tiempo cogieron a dos sátiros en los montes de Sajonia." Marasso explains the source of these strange quotations. They are a commonplace in mythological type books of the seventeenth and eighteenth centuries, in Baltasar Vitoria's *Teatro de los dioses de la gentilidad* (1670) and *Emblemata* by Alciato (1546). But Darío has taken almost literally from Padre Nieremberg's *Curiosa filosofía* (1630) a passage which refers to the monsters, with documentation of those quoted by Darío in "La ninfa" (Marasso, p. 356).

In the fantastic atmosphere of "El sátiro sordo" the figure of the satyr is ironically presented. He is a gross, savage-like creature, who, after being deafened by Apollo for having dared surprise the god of music while playing his lyre, remains impassive to the delicate songs of Philomela. This satyr is completely carnal: "Él permanecía impasible, o lanzaba sus carcajadas salvajes y saltaba lascivo y alegre cuando percibía por el ramaje lleno de brechas alguna cadera blanca y rotunda que acariciaba el sol con su luz rubia" (*CC*, 111). This satyr is the pursuer of nymphs, the "feliz bribón" who followed the advice of the gods: "Goza, el bosque es tuyo; sé un feliz bribón, persigue ninfas y suena tu flauta." Thus far, we have seen two points of reference pertaining to the satyr: the sensuality traditionally associated with him, which usually appears capriciously in Darío, and the legend of the real existence of these beasts.

Now we shall chronologically follow the development of the satyr's role in Darío's works after *Azul* .... In "Responso a Verlaine" (1896) the contradictory nature of Verlaine's soul is expressed in mythological terms:

De noche en la montaña, en la negra montaña
de las Visiones, pase gigante sombra extraña,
sombra de un Sátiro espectral;
que ella al Centauro adusto con su grandeza asuste; (*OPC*, 652)

[5] Guillermo Valencia relates the encounter of St. Anthony with a centaur in "San Antonio y el centauro" (1898). He here quotes from St. Jerome's *In vita sancti Pauli eremitae. cf. centauro.* Flaubert's widely read *La tentation de Saint Antoine* (1874) was surely an influence on both Darío and Valencia.

Here we have Verlaine as a satyr, purified in this moment of the supremacy of Christianity over his pagan instincts. The Satyr's soul will be within the harmony of the universe. The hybrid forces of disorder, the centaurs, will flee, frightened by the divine harmony. It is a triumph of Beauty over bestial and sensual elements, and the light of Salvation will shine:

> y el Sátiro contemple sobre un lejano monte
> una cruz que se eleva cubriendo el horizonte
> ¡y un resplandor sobre la cruz!

In "Coloquio de los centauros" (1896) the centaur Taumantes[6] expresses the concept of a primitive, maternal, protecting nature that attempts to explain monsters. The satyr joins the Apollonian with the Panic:

> El monstruo expresa un ansia del corazón del Orbe;
> en el centauro el bruto la vida humana absorbe;
> el sátiro es la selva sagrada y la lujuria,
> une sexuales ímpetus a la armoniosa furia.   (*OPC*, 633)

In "Dezir" (1896), however, the fascination with the sensuality of the "sátiro ladino" appears:

> que dió a mi labio sediento
> nuevo aliento,
> nueva copa y nuevo vino.   (*OPC*, 664)

There is a hedonistic exaltation of the satyr:

> ¡Bien haya el sátiro griego
> que me enseñó el dulce juego!
> En el reino de mi aurora
> no hay ayer, hoy ni mañana;
> danzo las danzas de ahora
> con la música pagana.   (*OPC*, 665)

But an implicit note of warning at the very end undoes the previous effect. Addressing himself to the beautiful lady who charmed him, the poet says:

---

[6] Eureto, Caumantes, Arneo and Hipea for Eurito, Taumantes, Areo and Hipasos are taken from Ovid's *Metamorphoses*, XII. The spelling is a result of errors in the translation of Sánchez de Viana (1590), found in the "Biblioteca Clásica."

> dió una negra perla rara
> Luzbel para
> tu diadema de locuras.   (*OPC*, 665)

The vacillation between the pagan and the Christian that is so characteristic of Darío is magnificently expressed in one stanza of "Yo soy aquel . . ." (1907):

> Bosque ideal que lo real complica;
> allí el cuerpo arde y vive y Psiquis vuela;
> mientras abajo el sátiro fornica,
> ebria de azul deslíe Filomela.   (*OPC*, 687)

In these complications of the ideal, Darío has found the expression of his philosophy, Pan and Psyche, the Satyr and Philomela. These lines seem, in part, to recall and amplify the idealistic pantheism of Hugo's "Le satyre:"

> Son caprice, à la fois divin et bestial,
> montait jusqu'au rocher sacré de l'idéal,
> car partout où l'oiseau vole, la chèvre y grimpe.

Darío's ideal forest is of a vital inspiration, for it unites the real to the ideal.

In "La cartuja" (1907) the satyr appears identified exclusively with sensuality in a simile in which Darío likens himself to the satyr:

> Darme otros ojos, no estos ojos vivos
> que gozan en mirar, como los ojos
> de los sátiros locos medio chivos,
> redondeces de nieve y labios rojos.   (*OPC*, 863)

This satyr is similar to the one in "Responso a Verlaine" that represented the domination of the pagan aspect of Verlaine's soul by the Christian.

The satyr of the "Responso" is again recalled in the story "Palimpsesto II" (1908), for here the satyr expresses the defeat of paganism as he talks to the centaur he has met. The satyr questions the validity of the centaur's automatic assumption that the divine being he saw in the guise of a "bello anciano" was Jupiter: "¿Tú ignoras acaso que una aurora nueva abre ya las puertas del Oriente y que los dioses todos han caído delante de otro Dios más fuerte y más grande?

El anciano que tú has visto no era Júpiter, no es ningún ser olímpico. Es un enviado del Dios nuevo" (*CC*, 289). He adds, and with no apparent regret, that times have changed for the satyrs. Their flutes do not sound as before and "a través de las hojas y ramajes no hemos visto una sola ninfa de rosa y mármol vivos como las que eran antes nuestro encanto." When the satyr met St. Anthony, the former, as the envoy of his comrades in search of God, pleaded with him to intercede in their behalf. Even the satyrs have recognized the ultimate truth: "La muerte nos persigue. Todos hemos tendidos nuestros brazos velludos y hemos inclinado nuestras pobres testas cornudas pidiendo amparo al que se anuncia como único Dios inmortal" (*CC*, 289).

Darío's subtle portrayal of the satyr is but one example of his vacillation between the pagan and the Christian. We shall explain in the next chapter whether this ambiguity is merely an alternate occurrence of pagan and Christian sentiments, as Darío criticism has maintained, or something more.

Satiresa (A modern feminine form morphologically similar to *faunesa*. Heredia wrote a poem called "La centauresse." *Centauresse* in Rimbaud's "Villes I." Marasso, p. 413: in Mendès. *Vampiresa* in the "Epístola a la señora de Leopoldo Lugones" and *diablesa* in the "Canto a la Argentina." Darío speaks of "mujeres-cisnesas" in "Por el Rhin.")

Darío saw female satyrs represented in art. René Ménard, in *Mythologie dans l'art ancien et moderne* (Paris, 1878), speaks of male and female satyrs. Clodion's "Satyre femelle" has goat's feet. All Darío tells us is that "Era una satiresa de mis fiestas paganas" (*OPC*, 673). The *satiresa* connotes a sensuality no less intense than that of the satyr:

> Tenemos carne de centauros
> y satiresas.   (*OPC*, 842)

(See *faunesa*.)

Centauro (Corominas: first documented in *Libros del saber de Astronomía* (1256-76). *Autoridades* gives several examples. Huerta's translation of Pliny (1629): "Galeno hace burla y se ríe de Píndaro poeta, por haver dicho que los Centauros eran hijos de hombres y de caballos." Diego Gracián's *Morales de Plutarcho* (1542): "Como no hai Centauros medio hombres y medio caballos." Solís' *Historia de la Nueva España* (1685): "Aprehendieron, con el primer assombro, que eran monstruos feroces, compuestos de hombre y bruto: al modo que menor disculpa creyó la Gentilidad sus Centauros." Also in Gracián's *Criticón* (1651-53 and 1657). *Centauro* is later documented in Moratín (hijo) according to the *Vocabulario* and in Valera (*DE*). Alfonso Rabbe wrote a poem in prose "Le centaure." Darío might well have known this composition when he wrote "Palimpsesto," published in 1892 with the title "Los centauros." Henri de Régnier's poems such as "Aréthuse" and "Dejanire" are filled with centaurs as are Maurice du Plessys and Maurice de Guérin's poems of the same title "Le centaure" and Heredia's "Fuite des centaures." *Centaure* is frequent in Flaubert's *La tentation* . . . and in Mendès's *Bacchus*.)

The centaurs, like the satyrs and many other mythological beings, were popular decorative elements in eighteenth-century France. The centaur is pictured in this way in "La ninfa," where Lesbia exalts their sensuality by proclaiming them even more desirable than the satyrs: "Yo quisiera dar vida a mis bronces, y si esto fuese posible, mi amante sería uno de esos velludos semidioses. Os advierto que más que a los sátiros adoro a los centauros; y que me dejaría robar por uno de esos monstruos robustos, sólo por oír las quejas del engañado, que tocaría su flauta lleno de tristeza." The centaurs, too, are lecherous characters, the would-be lovers of the nymphs. In the poem "Palimpsesto" (1896) reference is made to the famed abduction of one of Diana's nymphs while she was bathing. This incident, related by Ovid in his *Metamorphoses,* was celebrated in Renaissance art and in the works of LeSueur and Albani. In Darío:

> Silencio. Señas hace ligero
> el que en la tropa va delantero,
> porque a un recodo de la campaña
> llegan, en donde Diana se baña.   (*OPC,* 657)

(See *Diana.*) The centaur that kidnaps this nymph is described as a lovely, delicate creature:

> Es el más joven y es el más bello;
> su piel es blanca, crespo el cabello,
> los cascos finos, . . .   (*OPC,* 658)

This plastic portrayal of the abductor caused Rodó to pause and comment in his study on *Prosas profanas* that the young centur is "esbelto y pulcro como el Cillaris descrito por Ovidio, el Cillaris de las *Metamorfosis* cuya parte humana semejaba una estatua y a quien el poeta llama 'bello si cabe nombre de belleza en los monstruos.' . . . Tal es la escena, que me figuro como un bajorelieve de Scopas o de Fidias."

Both this episode in "Palimpsesto" and the one in the "Coloquio de los centauros" treat the same inexhaustible theme of the sculptured centaur that is so popular in Maurice de Guérin and French prose of the nineteenth century. In Guérin's work, the centaur Macarée tells Mélampe his life's story. He recalls in beautifully plastic images his mother's return to her family: "Quelquefois aussi, ma mère rentrait, environnée du parfum des vallées ou ruisselante des flots qu'elle fréquentait . . . . Ma mère rentrait, tantôt animée d'une joie profonde, et tantôt triste et traînante et comme blessée. La joie qu'elle rapportait se marquait de loin dans quelques traits de sa marche et s'épandait de ses regards." In the "Coloquio" the centaurs are again described as abductors of the nymphs:

> y de robustos músculos, brazos y lomos aptos
> para portar las ninfas rosadas en los raptos. (*OPC,* 628)

The centaurs Darío describes are not always the brutal, rough, ugly Homeric centaurs. They can be elegant, learned and correct as we see in the mysterious and philosophical "Coloquio de los centauros." It is fitting that Orpheus should say in "El sátiro sordo," "Canto . . . de los centauros gallardos," for Darío's centaurs are at times precisely that. However, in "Trébol" (1905) the centaur appears very much a monster, but one calmed by the pacifying power of beauty:

> ya al misterioso son del noble coro
> calma el Centauro sus grotescas iras. (*OPC,* 722)

In the "Dedicatoria" of the *Poema del otoño* (1907), the sensual nature of the centaur is emphasized:

> tenemos carne de centauros
> y satiresas.   (*OPC.* 842)

In the story "Palimpsesto II" (1908) the centaur weeps when informed by the satyrs of the existence of a new God. St. Paul explains these tears to St. Anthony as he tells him of his encounter that morning with the satyr and the centaur: "Pues el centauro ha llorado mitad por los dioses antiguos de Grecia y mitad por la nueva fe, sentenciado será a correr mientras viva sobre el haz de la tierra hasta que dé un salto portentoso y, en virtud de sus lágrimas, ascienda al cielo azul para quedar siempre luminoso en la maravilla de las constelaciones" (*CC,* 290). The centaur, in contrast with the satyr, is depicted as more of a beast in this story because of his reluctant attitude towards the dawning Christianity.

An adjective Darío uses to describe the centaur is *biforme.* (*Autoridades*: in the *Rimas* of Don Félix de Arteaga, who speaks of an "árbol biforme." Marasso, p. 403: "El hombre centauro también es de naturaleza biforme," Rémy de Gourmont, *Latin mystique.* "A los Sátyros los llamó biformes Stroza Pater," Vitoria, *Teatro de los dioses.* "El biforme hijo de Filira," Fernando de Herrera.)

In the "Coloquio de los centauros" Pholus uses this adjective as an epithet to *ixionida,* which refers to the centaurs, except Chiron, as sons of Ixion: "El biforme ixionida" (*OPC,* 630).

II Sylvan Deities

Dríada (Corominas: in modern usage the form *dríada* [*driada* in Darío] is perhaps more frequent than *dríade*; first documented in Garcilaso (1536). *Autoridades*: in Garcilaso's "Égloga II" and in Saavedra Fajardo's *República literaria* (post 1648). *Dríada* in Menéndez y Pelayo's "Cintra" (1875) and in his "Sáficas I" (1875). The compound *hamadríadas* is in Gutiérrez Nájera's *Odas breves* (1893). *Dryades* in

Musset,[7] Laprade, Leconte de Lisle's "Khirôn" and "Souvenir" and in Banville.)

In Darío, the *driadas,* gay nymphs of the trees, appear in a highly plastic scene in the previously quoted passage from "A un pintor:"

> Vamos a cazar colores,
> ilusión los bosques dan,
> las driadas brillan flores
> y alegría el egipán.   (*OPC,* 807)

They again appear, visualized from the plastic arts, in "Pórtico" (1896). Marasso sees "Bacanal (bajorrelieve del vaso Borghese)" pictured in Ménard as the inspiration for these verses:

> mientras se enlaza en un bajorrelieve
> a una driada ceñida de hiedra. (*OPC,* 641)

This in indeed one of those instances when Darío seems more inspired by the plastic arts than by any literary model. The dryads are evoked in commonplace images in Banville and Laprade's poetry.

In Laprade's "Les deux muses" the dryad is just another nymph being plagued by an amorous satyr, in this case, a faun:

> Sous l'écorce j'ai vu le Faune en embuscade
> De ses longs bras tortus enlacer la Dryade.

In Banville's "La voie lactée," "Phyllis" and "Clymène" they are referred to in the most stylized manner possible: "les Dryades des bois."

The "gaita gallega" accent of Darío's verse shows that he used the stress *driada,* not *dríada.* This form is perhaps by suggestion of the French and by analogy with the grave accent as in *Ilíada.*

Silvano (*Autoridades*: in Saavedra Fajardo's *República literaria.* In Nicolás Fernández de Moratín (*DE*), and in Menéndez y Pelayo (*Obras,* LXI, 113). Littré: in Chénier's

---

[7] Alfred de Musset, *Poésies,* Paris, 1867, II, 88.

Idylles, "L'Aveugle." *Sylvain* occurs frequently in Hugo's "Le satyre" as well as in Leconte de Lisle's "Glaucé," "La source" and "Hylas." In Verlaine's *Fêtes galantes:* "deux silvains hilares" and in Laprade and Banville.)

In Darío's "Un retrato de Watteau" (1887) a statue of a *silvano* serves to re-create the voluptuousness and elegance of eighteenth-century France as have the satyr and the centaur. The woman in her lavish boudoir smiles enigmatically, "quizá en recuerdo del amor galante, del madrigal recitado junto al tapiz de figuras pastoriles o mitológicas, o del beso a furto, tras la estatua de algún silvano, en la penumbra" (*CC,* 47). Darío's fascination with the voluptuous air evoked by these divinities does not include the sensual detail found in some of his models. In "Éleusis," for example, Laprade speaks of "Nymphes aux seins rougis des baisers des Sylvains."

These sylvan deities appear in Banville's "Les jardins" (1867) in a scene that foreshadows the smiling faun in *Fêtes galantes* (1869) who seems to prophesy an end to the merriment in those elaborate gardens. There is an enormous difference, though, for Banville's garden is already abandoned and strewn with passé marble adornments:

> Mais voici qu'à présent les rosiers chevelus
> Sont devenus broussaille et ne fleurissent plus;
> Le temps a fracassé le marbre blanc des urnes;
> Le rossignol a fui les chênes taciturnes;
> Les Nymphes de Coustou, les Sylvains et les Pans
> S'affaissent éperdus sous les lierres rampants;

The *silvano* recurs as an inanimate object in "Las razones de Ashavero" (1893). The poet will ponder the problem of obtaining the best form of government even though he is gravely occupied with "el epitalamio de un jazmín, la salutación a una ninfa y un epigrama para la estatua de un silvano."

Like Pan and Faunus, Silvanus came to constitute a polymorphic god and he gave to the dionysiac cortege many silvani, a fact that is clear from the above passages. In a pagan exaltation of the senses in the "Dedicatoria" of the *Poema del otoño* (1907) Darío evokes the numerous silvani with fervor:

89

¡Oh! Niña que con Eros juegas,
niños lozanos,
danzad con las ninfas griegas
y los silvanos.   (*OPC*, 839)

There is a similar gay sylvan scene in Laprade's "Les deux muses:" "J'ai surpris dans les bois la Nymphe et le Sylvain."

Fauno (Corominas: first documented in Alonso Fernández de Palencia (1490). *Autoridades*: in *La Crónica general* (1543), "Falláronlas los homes montesinos, que son llamados Sátyros e faunos" and in Espinel's *Vida del escudero Marcos de Obregón* (1618), "Estaba llena de cosas que ponía temor, como eran cabezas de demonios, de leones, de tigres, faunos y centauros." Alonso, *La lengua* . . ., p. 55: in *Don Quijote* (1605) and Góngora's *Soledad primera* (1611); word common among the Spanish Latinistic poets from the end of the fourteenth century to the beginning of the sixteenth. In Nicolás Fernández de Moratín (*DE*) and in Menéndez y Pelayo (*Obras*, LXI, 113, 115). *Faune* in Laprade, Flaubert's *La tentation* . . ., Sully Prudhomme's "La nature et la tradition" and in Mendès's *Bacchus*. Of course, there is Mallarmé's "L'après-midi d'un faune" and Verlaine's "Le faune.")

As we would now expect, many of Darío's fauns are statues. In the story "El palacio del sol" (1887) the pale, anemic child in her garden contrasts with the robustness of the faun: "Se apoyó en el zócalo de un fauno soberbio y bizarro que, húmedos de rocío sus cabellos de mármol, bañaba en luz su torso espléndido y desnudo" (*CC*, 36). The faun seems to come alive; when Berta leaves with the fairy, it is a "fauno orgulloso" who watches her depart, fresh and smiling. Similarly in "Arte y hielo" (1888) the sculptor inquires, "¿Gustáis de ese fauno sonriente que se muestra lleno de gallardía?" The previously alluded to faun-statue in *Fêtes galantes* suggests that the gaiety will pass:

Un vieux faune de terre cuite
Rit au centre des boulingrins,
Présageant sans doute une suite
Mauvaise à ces instants sereins.

The fauns, often portrayed dancing and leaping by the plastic arts, are presented in this fashion in Darío. In "El sátiro sordo," "danzaban coros de bacantes . . . y acompañando la armonía, . . . faunos adolescentes" (*CC*, 111). Darío's French models frequently present the fauns as part of the dionysiac entourage as they did the satyrs. In the second act of Mendès's *Bacchus* the *faunes,* accompanied by the *aegipans* and *satyres,* are intoxicated and leaping about playing their "tambours et sistres." A similar tone is evident in Laprade's "Symphonie des saisons:" "Voici le choeur des joyeux Faunes." On an amphora that is described in Darío's "Respecto a Horacio" we see "la figura de Sileno, que ríe viendo danzar un coro de faunos, los cuales levantan sobre sus cabezas sortijas de caireles y pámpanos recién cortados" (*CC*, 221). In "Pórtico" we have the pretext of a mythological painting:

> Toda desnuda, en los claros diamantes
> que en la Castalia recaman las ninfas,
> viéronla tropas de faunos saltantes,
> cual la más fresca y gentil de las ninfas. (*OPC*, 638)

The sensual nature of the faun is further underlined by identifying him as a nymph hunter:

> Un joven fauno robusto y violento,
> dulce terror de las ninfas incautas. (*OPC*, 641)

This common portrayal of the faun is seen in Laprade's "Les deux muses" in the passage quoted with reference to the dryads.

The faun, because of his inclinations, is a dangerous creature. Darío warns his son in "A Rubencito" not to heed the enticements of the faun: "No oigas al fauno extraordinario que su siringa suene." This verse is quite like a portion of Laprade's "Éleusis" both in lexicon and tone:

> Adieu les songes d'or qui pleuvent des vieux aunes,
> Les meutes d'Artémis et le syrinx des Faunes!

Mallarmé's "L'après-midi d'un faune" was also known to Darío. There is, however, a significant difference in each one's presentation of the faun. Mallarmé's poem is a monologue. The faun muses. Did it happen or did he dream that he had come upon a bevy of nymphs that fled into the water? Tired of trying to grasp anything so ethereal, the faun turns his fancies to the gross, attainable pleasures of the orgy that is sure to take place in the nearby woodland. Such sexual immediacy is absent in Darío.

Faunesa (Modern feminine form of *fauno,* morphologically analogous to *satiresa. Faunesse* in Banville's "Une femme de Rubens" (1867). Marasso, p. 406: title of a book by Feret (1886). Pierre Louÿs wrote "Les petites faunesses.")

In Darío the *faunesa* connotes the sensuality of her male counterpart. In "Ite, missa est" (1896) it is an unspiritual Darío who says:

Apagará la llama de la vestal intacta
¡y la faunesa antigua me rugirá de amor! (*OPC*, 627)

Darío advises his son to avoid not only the temptation of the faun's music, but also the call of the equally dangerous *faunesa*: "No oigas a la faunesa que te lanza su grito" (*OPC,* 1012).

III   *Aquatic Divinities*

Delfín (Corominas: first documented in the *Cancionero de Baena* (1445). *Autoridades*: in Calvete de la Estrella's *Viaje del rey Felipe II* (1552) and in Huerta's translation of Pliny. Also in Francisco de la Torre, Quintana (*Poesías,* p. 158), Valera (*Obras,* XII, 88, 110) and in Menéndez y Pelayo (*Obras,* LXI, 48). *Dauphin* in Gautier, Banville and in Sully Prudhomme's "La néréide.")

The *delfín* does not appear often in Darío's works. These creatures, benevolent to sailors, usually are companions of the tritons in a manner that recalls the paintings of Albani and Boucher. At Venus' birth in the "Coloquio de los centauros," her cortege is comprised of "tritónicas melenas y dorsos de delfines" that decidedly resemble those in Boucher's

"Birth of Venus."[8] Similarly, the dolphins are Venus' attendants in Banville's "Une femme de Rubens:"

> C'est l'ange Cythérée
> Dans la mer azurée
> Appuyant ses pieds fins
> Sur les dauphins.

In Gautier's "Les néréides" the dolphins are part of a plastic grouping of nymphs and tritons:

> Et les dauphins, arquant leurs croupes,
> D'Arion attendaient l'appel.

In "Un retrato de Watteau" (1887) the *delfín* appears in an equally plastic image, but as an article of adornment as do "les dauphins de marbre" in Banville's "La fontaine de jouvence." In Darío, "en el plafón en forma de óvalo va por el fondo inmenso y azulado, sobre el lomo de un toro robusto y divino, la bella Europa, entre delfines áureos y tritones corpulentos" (*CC,* 47). The capitalization of this word in "Fugitiva" (1892) is perhaps to distinguish the sea divinity from *Delfín* 'royal princess:' "es reina, princesa, Delfín o hada" (*CC,* 158).

Tritón (*Autoridades*: in Lope's *Arcadia* (1598) and Saavedra Fajardo's *República literaria*: "Dando a creer que había en el mar Tritones, Phocas y Neréidas." Also in Meléndez Valdés,[9] Moratín (*Voc.*), and in Menéndez y Pelayo (*Obras,* LXI, 166). *DRAE,* 1956: the common noun < sea god Triton. The whole idea of the sea god multiplied in Greek fantasy, and as the earth became populated with sileni and fauns, so did the sea with tritons. *Tritons* in Gautier's "Les néréides," Laprade's "Les deux muses," Flaubert's *La tentation*... and in Banville.)

As Darío grouped the dolphins and tritons, so he does with the tritons and sirens. The multiplicity of the tritons is

---

[8] See Marasso, *op. cit.,* for a reproduction of this scene from Ménard's book. This is but one indication of the numerous similarities between Darío's poetry and a scene in Ménard.

[9] Meléndez Valdés, *Odas anacreónticas y otros poemas,* Barcelona, 1944, p. 177.

alluded to in "Marina" (1905), a poem that recalls Europa's abduction. The bull's roar is likened to the commotion caused by the tritons, as in the "Coloquio de los centauros." In "Marina:"

> Magnífico y sonoro
> le oye en las aguas como
> un tropel de tropeles,
> ¡tropel de los tropeles de tritones! (*OPC,* 734)

The turmoil of the introductory scene of the "Coloquio de los centauros" is in contrast with the sudden calm and solemnity brought about to discuss the mysterious nature of things. In recognition of this event, even the capricious tritons still their noise: "Calladas las bocinas a los tritones gratas" (*OPC,* 628). This occurs on the island where "el tritón erige su caracol sonoro." (See *Tritón.*) The tritons as attendants of Venus, in the manner of Boucher's painting, also captured Banville's fancy. In "Songe d'hiver" we have a plastic picture of

> La Vénus Aphrodite ou l'Anadyomène,
> Caressant les cheveux d'un triton qui la mène.

Darío again alludes to the real existence of certain mythological beings in "Retorno" (1906):

> ¡y cuántas [veces] he mirado tropeles de tritones
> y cortejos de ninfas ceñidas de azahares! (*OPC,* 904)

Sirena (Corominas: first documented in Spanish in the *Cancionero de Baena* as *serena. Sirena,* according to Corominas, is found in Alonso Fernández de Palencia (1490). *Autoridades*: in Villamediana's *La gloria de Niquea* (1629). Also in Francisco de la Torre (*Poesías,* p. 130), Moratín (*Voc.*), Valera (*Obras,* X, 8) and Menéndez y Pelayo (*Obras,* LXII, 72). In Gautier, Laprade, Leconte de Lisle, Flaubert's *La tentation* . . ., Sully Prudhomme's "La néréide," Mallarmé (*Poésies,* p. 7), Heredia (*Poésies,* p. 2) and in Samain.)

In keeping with a long tradition, Darío proclaims the real existence of these beings:

> ¡Oh, cuántas veces, cuántas veces oí los sones
> de las sirenas líricas en los clásicos mares! (*OPC,* 904)

Covarrubias tells us, "Plinio dize que no es fabuloso el aver en la mar tritones y nereydas que tienen forma de hombre y de mujer" (p. 941). This notion was widespread. Above all, though, the legend of the "sirenas de labios escarlatas" as singers of a sweet song that lured sailors to their doom has attracted poets. This tale was popularized through the incident of Ulysses having his crew's ears filled with wax and himself tied to the mast so he could safely hear that "Choeur fatal et divin" that Samain describes in "Les sirènes." It is this aspect of the sirens as cruel temptresses that Silvestre dwells on in his commentary on Rodin's sculpture.[10] Similarly, Laprade points up the treachery of the sirens in "Les argonautes:"

> C'est l'île de Circé, c'est l'antre des Syrènes;
> Leur chanson va tenter vos coeurs!

On the other hand, the seductive song of the sirens triumphs in Laprade's "Symphonie des saisons:"

> Venez écouter de plus près
> La douce voix de la Sirène.

In Leconte de Lisle's "Glaucé" the sirens prove resistible:

> Ni les baisers promis, ni les voix de sirène
> N'ont troublé de mon coeur la profondeur sereine.

Darío, in his "Epístola" to Madame Lugones (1907), pictures himself reposing after a lifelong struggle against the enticements of the sirens:

> Hay en mí un griego antiguo que aquí descansó un día
> después que le dejaron loco de melodía
> las sirenas rosadas que atrajeron su barca. (*OPC*, 818)

Hopefully addressing "¡Torres de Dios!" (1905), he predicts the end of the sirens:

> La mágica esperanza anuncia un día
> en que sobre la roca de armonía
> expirará la pérfida sirena.
> Esperad, esperemos todavía. (*OPC*, 701)

[10] Armand Silvestre, *La sculpture aux salons*, Paris, 1896, pp. 121-124. The emphasis is on sensual detail, a tone common in Silvestre. See Peyre, *L'influence des littératures antiques*, p. 69.

Darío goes beyond this traditional portrayal of the siren. There is a fanciful inversion of the myth of the seductive song of the sirens in "Al partir Mayorga Rivas." The sirens will be the victims of a song more enchanting than their own:

> La sal del mar en nuestras venas
> irán, sin canto seductor,
> embelesadas por el suave
> cántico tuyo, ¡oh gran cantor! (*OPC*, 1032)

In the story "La pesca" (1896) the sirens surprise us by stepping out of their treacherous role. They are benevolent creatures: "mi red conocida y querida de los tritones y de las sirenas" (*CC*, 250). The concept of their charming voice is extended to eulogize in "Pórtico" (1896) the popular songs sung by the "labios quemantes de humanas sirenas." In the "Dedicatoria" of the *Poema del otoño* we see the depth of Darío's mythological portrayals. The sensual aspect of the sirens is implied as part of the broader concept of man as a microcosmos:

> . . . .
>
> en nosotros corre la savia
> del Universo.
>
> Nuestro cráneo guarda el vibrar
> de tierra y sol,
> como el ruido de la mar
> el caracol.
>
> La sal del mar en nuestras venas
> va a borbotones;
> tenemos sangre de sirenas
> y de tritones. (*OPC*, 842)

In "Véspera" (1907) the result of the contemplation of Venus-star is a mixture of emotions, of the pure and the sensual. On looking at her, the poet hears "o son de lira, o canto de sirena" (*OPC*, 845).

The sirens, too, appear as voluptuous and elegant adornments in Darío. This is the portrayal that also intrigued his French models. Gautier exhorts the artist in "L'Art:"

96

> Fais les sirènes bleues,
> Tordant de cent façons
> Leurs queues,
> Les monstres des blasons;

Samain creates an even more plastic picture of these creatures coquettishly twisting their tails in "Les sirènes" as they do in Gautier's "Caerulei Oculi." In Samain:

> Diaphanes blancheurs dans la nuit émergeant,
> Les Sirènes venaient, lentes, tordant leurs queues
> Souples, et sous la lune, au long des vagues bleues,
> Roulaient et déroulaient leurs volutes d'argent.

In "Arte y hielo" the sculptor boasts, "Para vosotras, queridas mujeres, haré sátiros y sirenas que serán la joya de vuestro tocador." In "Un retrato de Watteau," "en el ansa de un jardín de Rouen lleno de agua perfumada, le tiende los brazos y los pechos una sirena con la cola corva y brillante de escamas argentinas" (*CC*, 47).

Náyade (Corominas: *náyade* is first documented in Calvete de Estrella (1552). We might predate this word from information found in *Autoridades* with reference to the existence of *dríada* in Bachiller de la *Torre* (1440). However, the lines quoted are actually from Francisco de la Torre's "Égloga II" (1631): "Dríadas bellas, Náyades del río, / Compañía de Oréadas serena, / Fieles testigos de mi gran llanto." In Moratín (*Voc.*), Valera (*Romances,* p. 100), Bécquer, Menéndez y Pelayo (*Obras,* LXI, 152, 185) and Gutiérrez Nájera.[11] *Naïade* in Musset (*Poésies,* p. 65), Laprade, Leconte de Lisle, Banville, Mallarmé (*Poésies,* p. 67) and in Sully Prudhomme.)

In Darío's description of the naiads, we again see how aware he is of the various traditions and details associated with the divinities. For example, the naiads, known to be fond of music, are capriciously presented in "El sátiro sordo." The potency of Orpheus' music is charmingly corroborated by the

---

[11] Gustavo Adolfo Bécquer, *Rimas,* Madrid, 1936, p. 56. *Manuel Gutiérrez* Nájera, *Poesías completas,* ed. Francisco González Guerrero, México, 1953, II, 295. Future quotations from these books will be given in the text.

naiad's response: "Una náyade virgen a quien nunca ni una sola mirada del sátiro había profando, se acercó tímida al cantor y le dijo: 'yo te amo' " (*CC*, 114). The reference "virgen" alludes to the fact that the naiads were also the priestesses of Bacchus. The same characterization of the naiad is seen in "Responso a Verlaine;" Darío expresses the hope that even the virginal naiad will be filled with the mixed emotions of passion and fear at the mere mention of Verlaine's name:

> y que la virgen náyade, cuando ese nombre escuche,
> con ansias y temores entre las linfas luche
> llena de miedo y de pasión. (*OPC*, 652)

The naiad remains unmoved by Terminus' smile in "La Dea" (1896). Here, her virtues are emphasized all the more by the symbols of terrestrial life around her:

> Término su sonrisa de piedra brinda en vano
> a la desnuda náyade y a la ninfa hechicera
> que viene a la soberbia fiesta de la pradera
> y del boscaje, en busca del lírico Silvano. (*OPC*, 650)

In "La source" Banville presents her also as "La vierge, la Naïade argentine . . . . " However, Banville seems more captivated with her than Darío ever was, for Banville credits her with a supernatural power over nature that recalls a description in "La cithare." In "La source:"

> La petite Naïade est pensive. Elle rit.
> Devant ses pieds d'ivoire un narcisse fleurit.
> Oiseaux, ne chantez pas; taisez-vous, brises folles,
> Car elle est votre joie, ailes, brises, corolles,
> Verdures! Le désert, épris de ses yeux bleus,
> Écoute murmurer dans le roc sourcilleux
> Son flot que frange à peine une légère écume.
> L'aigle laisse tomber à ses pieds une plume
> En ouvrant dans l'éther son vol démesuré;
> L'alouettte vient boire au bassin azuré
> Dont son aile timide agite la surface.

The naiads, in contrast with the sirens, are fun-loving and fond of playing games. In Leconte de Lisle's "Hélène" they appear in a traditional pose: "Les Naïades riaient dans les claires fontaines." Darío pictures them as frolicsome creatures in "Carta del país azul" (1888), but enveloped in an air of sensuality in a dionysiac exaltation of Pan: "Y amo a Pan porque, como yo, es aficionado a la música y a los sonoros ditirambos, junto a los riachuelos armoniosos, donde triscan las náyades, la cadera sobre la linfa, el busto al aire, todas sonrosadas al beso fecundo y ardiente del gran sol" (CC, 68). These naiads resemble "l'invitante Naïade" in Laprade's "Les deux muses." In "Canción" (1896) the naiads, traditionally portrayed in art as crowned with flowers, fittingly salute the goddess of flowers:

> y en la matutina hora
> de la clara fuente mana
> la salutación pagana
> de las náyades a Flora.   (OPC, 667)

Ninfa (D. Alonso, *La lengua* . . ., p. 60: in Juan de Mena; first appears in Góngora in 1582. *Ninfa* later in Francisco de la Torre (*Poesías*, pp. 1, 16, 24, 29), Moratín (*Voc.*), Bello (*Poesías*, pp. 22, 179), commonly in Valera's translations and original works as in (*Romances*, pp. 72, 99, 262, 286), Menéndez y Pelayo (*Obras*, LXI, 115-117, 139, 152), and in Gutiérrez Nájera (*Poesías*, II, 267, 272, 275, 285). Also in Musset (*Poésies*, p. 64), Gautier, Laprade, Leconte de Lisle, Flaubert's *La tentation* . . ., Banville, Mallarmé (*Poésies*, p. 43) and in Sully Prudhomme's "La néréide" and "Silène.")

Like the satyrs, Darío's nymphs represent intense sensuality. However, the tone surrounding the nymphs is distinct. It is a joy in the mere contemplation of them:

> La ninfa junto a la fuente pasa
> y tiene en su blancura
> lo que inspira, lo que dura,
> lo que aroma y lo que abrasa. (OPC, 998)

Darío, like many of his models, delights in describing the nymphs. Leconte de Lisle presents them in straightforward, highly plastic images. In "La source" there is a nymph "au corps de neige." In "Khirôn" she is further described as "la Nymphe aux blonds cheveux." In "Les plaintes du cyclope" she is pursued in vain: "Et suppliait la Nymphe au coeur frivole et dur." In a poem to Th. Gautier in *Odelettes,* Banville proclaims him "l'amant des Nymphes de marbre." Indeed, Gautier, in whose works there is no abundance of secondary divinities, finds the nymphs a beautiful subject, judging from a scene he paints in "Les néréides:"

> Sur l'écume blanche qui frange
> Le manteau glauque de la mer
> Se groupent en bouquet étrange
> Trois nymphes, fleurs du gouffre amer.
>
> Comme des lis noyés, la houle
> Fait dans sa volute d'argent
> Danser leurs beaux corps qu'elle roule,
> Les élevant, les submergeant.

As the title clearly implies, Gautier is speaking of the nereids, who were sea nymphs. *Nymph* is, of course, a generic name for a large number of female divinities who were distinguished according to the spheres of nature with which they were connected.

In Laprade's "Les deux muses" the nymphs connote beauty and desirability in a plastic scene depicting a whole group of the lesser divinities:

> J'ai surpris dans les bois la Nymphe et le Sylvain.
> Sous l'écorce j'ai vu le Faune en embuscade
> De ses longs bras tortus enlacer la Dryade.
> Les tritons argentés, les nymphes aux yeux verts,
> Souriant aux pêcheurs, s'ébattent sur les mers.

In Banville's "Pour Mademoiselle" from *Les stalactites* the nymphs, viewed as objects of art, are identified with the Bacchic rites:

> Amours des bas-reliefs, ô Nymphes et Bacchantes,
> Qui, sur l'Ida nocturne, au bruit d'un tambourin,
> Les fronts échevelés en tresses provocantes,
> Dansiez en agitant vos crotales d'airain!

A good bit of the nymphs' time is spent fleeing the lecherous fauns and satyrs. In "El velo de la reina Mab" (1887): "Amo los desnudos en que la ninfa huye y el fauno tiende los brazos" (*CC*, 52). Again in *"Pórtico"* the nymph is faced with the same problem:

> Un joven fauno robusto y violento,
> dulce terror de las ninfas incautas. (*OPC*, 641)

For the most part, though, the nymph escapes her aspiring seducer, fleeing to the forest of the deaf satyr, "donde ninfas y bacantes eran siempre acariciadas y siempre vírgenes" (*CC*, 113). Very few of Darío's nymphs are anything less than the "inviolada ninfa" who hides in fright from Atis' shout in "Friso." Traditionally, the nymphs are thought of as the "Nymphes pures" that Banville describes in "Inviolata." There is, however, the boast of the old gnome in "El rubí" (1888), "caí a un lago donde violé a una ninfa" and the nymph from Diana's cortege who was abducted by Pholus in "Palimpsesto" (1896):

> En un instante, veloz y listo,
> a una tan bella como Calisto,
> ninfa que a la alta diosa acompaña,
> saca de la onda donde se baña. (*OPC*, 658)

At times there is an intentional ambiguity in Darío's evocations of the nymphs that proves very effective both in his prose and his poetry. In "Eros" Darío says, "En cada mujer miro como una ninfa griega." There is a constant equation of *mujer* and *ninfa,* whereby the image of woman is powerfully exalted. The old gnome in "El rubí" tells what he saw in a field one day as he left the cavern:

> Brazos, espaldas, senos desnudos, azucenas,
> rosas, panecillos de marfil coronados de cerezas;
> ecos de risas áureas, festivas; y allá, entre
> espumas, entre las linfas rotas, bajo las
> verdes ramas . . .

> — ¿Ninfas?
> — No, mujeres. (*CC*, 83)

101

Darío might well have had in mind the parallel line from Rimbaud's "Phrases:" "Nymphes d'Horace coiffées au Premier Empire."

The whole problem, planted in jest in "La ninfa," is whether nymphs really exist. The answer is that they do, as beautiful as those created by myth and poetry, but nymphs of flesh and bone. Of course, one is reminded of Verlaine's delightful equivocation: "Est-elle en marbre ou non, la Vénus de Milo?" In Gautier's "Fantaisies d'hiver" there is a similar ambiguous air:

> Les femmes passent sous les arbres
> En martre, hermine et menu-vair,
> Et les déesses, frileux marbres,
> Ont pris aussi l'habit d'hiver.
>
> La Vénus Anadyomène
> Est en pelisse à capuchon;
> Flore, que la brise malmène,
> Plonge ses mains dans son manchon.

However, in the "Balada en honor de las musas de carne y hueso" Darío proclaims that: "¡La mejor musa es la de carne y hueso!"

Somewhat like the naiads, the nymphs appear as merry-makers in "Primaveral" (1888):

> donde se bañan desnudas
> las blancas ninfas que juegan, (*OPC*, 570)

Again in "Palimpsesto" (1896):

> Se oye el ruido de claras linfas
> y la algazara que hacen las ninfas. (*OPC*, 659)

In Sully Prudhomme's "Silène" the nymphs are thoroughly amused by Silenus' tipsy state, for "L'essaim des nymphes rit sur le rideau des cieux." The gaiety and sensuality suggested by the nymphs reappears in the "Dedicatoria" of the *Poema del otoño*. In a lyric exaltation of life and the senses Darío urges:

¡Oh! Niña que con Eros juegas,
niños lozanos,
danzad con las ninfas griegas
y los silvanos. (*OPC,* 839)

However, in the story "Palimpsesto II" (1908) the satyr
points out that times are changing in face of the dawning
Christianity, for "no hemos visto una sola ninfa de rosa y
mármol vivos como las que eran antes nuestro encanto" (*CC,*
289).

The phrase "ninfa de rosa" requires us to consider the
implications of its frequency in Darío's works. The image
"ninfa de rosa" and several variants such as "dedos de rosa"
and "brazos de rosa" are extremely common in Darío. He
knew Baráibar's translation of Anacreon's "Ode I" in which
we find, "Los brazos de las ninfas / y los dedos del alba /
son de rosa . . ." Compare the following passages from Darío.
In "Historia de un picaflor," "palmas rosadas"; in "Bouquet,"
"De rosa son hechos los brazos de las ninfas y los dedos de la
aurora"; in "La muerte de la emperatriz de la China," "dedos
de rosa" and "las blandas manos de rosa"; in "Febea," "las
más adorables manos rosadas"; in "Primaveral," "las tuyas
[manos] de rosa y seda." These are most likely influences
of Anacreon. Less certain, however, are those images that
seem to be a blend of Anacreon's ode and the *Aeneid,* I, 402:
"Dixit, et avertens rosea cervice refulsit . . . ." I have separated
the following examples from those that seem a more certain
influence of Anacreon on the basis that they have as much
in common with the Virgilian line: *rosa* or *rosada.* They do
not refer to *brazos* or *dedos* as in the ode by Anacreon. Some
are "muchacha fresca y rosada" in "El pájaro azul;" "cuerpos
de rosa y nieve" in "El velo de la reina Mab;" "aquella mu-
chachita de carne rosada" in "La muerte de la emperatriz de
la China;" "hecha de nieve y rosa nació la Anadiomena" in
"Coloquio de los centauros." There are, however, those instances that do seem clearly to recall the description of Venus'
rosy neck. (See *incessu patuit dea.*)

Yet, it is necessary to point out that similar, and some-

103

times identical images, were highly common in Darío's models. In Gautier's "La nue" an ethereal Venus is described thus:

> Et l'aurore répand des roses
> Sur son épaule de satin.

In Laprade's *Psyché* we find "Les Nymphes de la mer lavent ses pieds de rose" as well as ". . . descend l'aurore aux pieds de rose." In Leconte de Lisle's "Odes anacréontiques" there is the verse "La bouche et le sein des Nymphes sont roses!" in Banville's "L'exil des dieux" we find

> Aphroditè, marchant pieds nus (et son talon
> A la blancheur d'un astre et l'éclat d'une rose!)

She is the epitome of beauty "Avec son sein de rose et ses blancheurs d'étoile." In "Invitation" Samain writes, "L'aurore en son cristal baigne ses pieds rosés."

Certainly Homer deserves first credit for speaking of the rosy-fingered dawn. We know that Darío read the Hermosilla translation of the *Iliad*. As for the Virgilian influence, he had at hand the Caro translation, which is, along with Baráibar's translation of Anacreon, in the "Biblioteca Clásica." As a matter of fact, we believe that Anacreon is the best explanation of those images in Darío that are not closer to Virgil's line describing Venus' neck. Mejía Sánchez (pp. 260-261) discusses the great pleasure Darío took in displaying his knowledge of Anacreon. Darío's use of the word *barbiton,* thus far explained only in terms of Baráibar's translation of Anacreon, is strong indication of Darío's awareness of this poet. However, the diffusion of like images in writers Darío knew proves further that at times Darío's sources are so involved that it is impossible to be certain of his inspiration. At one point Darío himself was not completely sure of his indebtedness. In the *Historia de mis libros* he says, "En el cuento 'El rey burgués' creo reconocer la influencia de Daudet." For the most part, there is a happy blending of models in Darío.

Pegaso (*Autoridades*: In Saavedra Fajardo's *República literaria,* "Dando a creer que había en el aire Hypogryphos, Pegasos" and in Villaviciosa's *La mosquea* (1615). Littré: in Fr. Maynard. Also in Banville's "Andromède," Heredia's "Andromède au monstre" and "Persée et Andromède." Pierre Louÿs wrote a poem "Pégase." Marasso, p. 194: Pegasus as the winged horse of the poet dates back only to the Renaissance, according to Saglio.)

From the body of Medusa sprang Pegasus. After the slaughter of Medusa, Perseus mounted Pegasus and flew far and wide, coming at last to the realm of Atlas. Perseus wished merely to rest, but Atlas fearfully recalled a phophesy that a son of Jove would attempt to rob him of his golden apples. Perseus, finding Atlas too strong for him, held up the Gorgon's head, and Atlas was changed into stone. With this as his frame of reference, Banville says in "Andromède:"

> Mais Persée aux beaux yeux, le meurtrier d'Atlas,
> Vient et fend l'air, monté sur le divin Pégase.

Darío evokes Pegasus in several images that seem largely a display of erudition. For the most part, Pegasus is the inspiration of the poet. In "Pórtico" we find "listo y piafante su excelso pegaso." In "Misterioso" this winged horse is the basis for a eulogy of Antonio Machado:

> Montado en un raro Pegaso,
> un día al imposible fué.   (*OPC,* 808)

In "Pegaso" (1905) Darío, speaking of the divine character of poetry, glorifies his own poetic genius. He describes Pegasus as "ese caballo rudo y tembloroso." There is a noteworthy similarity between Darío's portrayals and the pictures of Pegasus in Ménard (figs. 347-353). Our poet boasts, "y yo, fuerte, he subido donde Pegaso pudo." He further describes himself as the "domador del corcel de cascos de diamante" (*OPC,* 699). A coin shown in Ménard depicts Bellerophon subduing the horse until then indomitable. In "Helios" (1905) the effects of Helios-Apolo are described with reference to Pegasus' flight:

> . . . Tiemblan las cumbres
> de los montes más altos
> que en sus rítmicos saltos
> tocó Pegaso, . . . (*OPC*, 703)

In "¡Carne, celeste carne de la mujer!" (1905) we are told that poetry will soar to extraordinary heights, inspired by the sight of nude Venus:

> Cuando el áureo Pegaso
> en la victoria matinal se lanza
> con el mágico ritmo de su paso
> hacia la vida y hacia la esperanza,
> si alza la crin y las narices hincha
> y sobre las montañas pone el casco sonoro
> y hacia la mar relincha,
> y el espacio se llena
> de un gran temblor de oro,
> es que ha visto desnuda a Anadiomena. (*OPC*, 731)

In the "Preludio" to Chocano in *El canto errante* (1907), Pegasus does not soar gracefully or move with "mágico ritmo" as he did above. On the contrary:

> (¡El Pegaso da saltos!)
>
> .   .   .   .
>
> Pegaso está contento. Pegaso piafa y brinca,
> porque Pegaso pace en los prados del inca. (*OPC*, 809)

In "Canto a la Argentina" (1910) Pegasus is identified with the glory of Buenos Aires:

> ¡Buenos Aires, amada ciudad,
> el Pegaso de estrellas herrado
> sobre ti vuela en vuelo inspirado!

Cíclope (*Autoridades*: in Calderón's *Apolo y Climena*. In Moratín (*Voc.*), Valera (*Romances,* p. 277) and Menéndez y Pelayo (*Obras*, LXII, 62). Littré: in a letter of Voltaire, 1773. Also in Laprade, Leconte de Lisle's "Les plaintes du cyclope," Flaubert's *La tentation* . . . and in Mendès's *Bacchus*.

According to Darío's essay on Poe in *Los raros,* Groussac described New York City policemen as "cíclopes.")

Darío seems to subscribe to the most common theory of the occupation of the cyclops. Hesiod's version of them as slaves of Jupiter in a subterranean cavern, forgers of the thunderbolt that killed Aesculapius, has been amplified upon by poets and artists. This role is confirmed by Virgil in the *Aeneid,* VIII, 424: "Ferreum exercebant vasto Cyclopes in antro." In *Psyché* Laprade refers to their subterranean habitat in an exhortation to the various mythological beings to regain their rightful place:

> Des vieux chênes, des flots, des antres souterrains,
> Dieux, ministres de l'Être, ô Cyclopes, Sylvains,
> Nymphes, Zéphyrs, Tritons, dieux légers, dieux énormes,
> Esprits universels qui supportez les formes:
> Rentrez dans votre ciel, dieux exilés là-bas!

In the pictorial essay "Aguafuerte" (1887) we are presented with the highly plastic image of "una muchacha blanca" at the entrance to the forge where the workers are employed. Her whiteness contrasts with the soot and carbon of the black cavern where the laborers ".... al resplandor de las llamaradas, tenían tallas de cíclopes" (*CC,* 44). An allusive reference to the industrious cyclops is made in "La cabeza," where we see a poet whose mind is crammed with sonnets, sounds and colors: "Resonaban en las concavidades de aquel cerebro martilleos de cíclope" (*CC,* 45).

Titánico (*DRAE,* 1956: 'Pertaining to Titans.' In Greek mythology, the children of Uranus and Gaea. *Titánico* first appears in the 1884 ed. of *DRAE.* Analogous morphological forms cited by Plowert in his *Petit glossaire* are *adamique* and *panique* in Verlaine and *édénique* in Jules Laforgue. *Titan* in Laprade, Flaubert's *La tentation* . . ., Banville's "Le festin des dieux" and in Sully Prudhomme's "Les écuries d'augias." Compare *pandórica* and *pánico* in the next chapter.)

In Darío this adjective, which means pertaining to or having the strength of the Titans, is used metaphorically to describe Lugones' poetic genius in "Pequeño poema de carnaval" (1907): "Juzga este ser titánico . . ." (*OPC*, 864). In *Psyché* Laprade recalls the Titans as the losers in the battle against Jupiter. Now, though, all is well:

> Et vous, Titans, l'Olympe est ouvert sans combats!
> Entre les dieux rivaux, toute haine s'oublie.

The Greco-Roman vocabulary that, to such a large extent, has been viewed as the result of Darío's Parnassian and symbolist readings is by no means exclusive indication of a "galicismo mental." Several of these words are well-documented in Spanish not only in the Golden Age, but often earlier and right through the eighteenth and nineteenth centuries. This fact, then, considerably modifies the idea that Darío was awakened to these "new words" by his modern French readings. On the contrary, the long history of these words in Spanish emphasizes the fact that Darío had a wealth of background upon which to draw. A great part of his genius was that he could assimilate this diverse background and interweave it with skill in his compositions. Surely the over-all atmosphere is that of the eighteenth-century France that came from his French readings. However, let us not establish Darío as a mere follower of the Parnassians.

One of the striking differences is that Darío does not reflect the smilingly permissive attitude towards sexual matters described by the Goncourt brothers. The heavily sensual details seen in Laprade, Silvestre and Mallarmé, furthermore, do not exist in Darío's works. Such erotic detail was not compatible with his personal taste and is, therefore, rejected. This artistic independence of Darío's is all the more impressive considering how fraught with sexual overtones many of these mythological figures are.

Most of Darío's images in which these divinities appear are highly plastic. In fact, there are many times when his images seem more likely the result of having seen a similar portrayal on a vase or in a painting than a reworking of an idea inspired by any literary model. The most superficial glance at René Ménard's book reveals that it was a profitable source of inspiration for Darío. Much of the poetry of his French models was plastic, too. Darío's plasticity, however, is unique in that his images are not just straightforward presentations of the myths. He usually brings these plastic portrayals to life. Even his evocations of eighteenth-century French art are animated in this way. At times Darío's vitalized portrayal of mythological scenes is delightfully fantastic or capricious; consider the story "El sátiro sordo." As Salinas so admirably pointed out, Darío's poetry has a tremendously vital urge. The consequence is a happy one, for Darío achieves a level of distinction in his mythological portrayals that is not reached by his French models. The very forces that drive Darío, his limitless joy in living and his fear of death, are often expressed in pagan terms. In "Dezir" (1896):

> En el reino de mi aurora
> no hay ayer, hoy ni mañana;
> danzo las danzas de ahora
> con la música pagana.

On other occasions we see the underlying fear of death in his vitalized mythology. It was a terror that mounted with the years as his mythological evocations decreased. Like the satyr in "Palimpsesto II" Darío knows all too well that "La muerte nos persigue." That many mythological figures come to express the Christianity of our poet will be even more evident in the next chapter. In the best sense of the word, Darío "exploits" all the possible meanings of these personalities. Such is not the case with his French models, who, for the most part, give us a highly stylized view of these mythological figures. Darío proves himself to be an artist in his prose as well as in his poetry by the way in which he makes the ancient myths his very own. With unsurpassed charm and imagination, he brings them to present times, distinguishing himself by the new vitality he infuses into them. The resultant tone is more "grecolatinizante" than "grecolatinista."

CHAPTER V

THE GREAT DIVINITIES

The poetic stimulus of the Greco-Roman world upon Darío's imagination is indisputable.[1] In that past civilization he found such fresh elements of beauty as the nymphs, who acquire extraordinarily pictorial meaning in "Acuarela" and "Era un aire suave." The atmosphere of fauns and satyrs constitutes an erotic climate that arouses his creative impulse, "donde los deseos de sus sentidos se verán rodeados de estímulos y ejemplos bellísimos y podrán medrar mejor que abandonados a sí mismos."[2] The elegant, erotic, hedonistic and frivolous tones of the era of *Azul* . . . and *Prosas profanas,* exemplified thus far in the lesser divinities, give way toward 1897 to more reflective moods, contemplations of life, death and religion. We shall see in further detail that around this year Darío's mythology takes on a marked Christian tone.[3]

[1] His fondness for Greco-Roman motifs does not, however, exclude others. In "Divagación" he speaks of "un amor florentino," "un amor alemán," "un amor de España," "amores exóticos" of China and Japan, and "amor hindú." In "Por el Rhin" and "Divagación" he mentions Lorelei and the "divino Heine." In "La muerte de la emperatriz de la China" he also uses Wagnerian motifs; Elsa and Lohengrin become the symbols of perfect love. The story "A las orillas del Rhin" unfolds in a medieval setting. The Germanic poetic and mythological world, like the Greco-Roman, reached Darío through French literature according to Ernesto Mejía Sánchez, *Los primeros cuentos de Rubén Darío,* México, 1951, pp. 23-29.

[2] Salinas, *La poesía de Rubén Darío,* p. 82.

[3] This is the first presentation of Darío's works from this point of view. Arturo Capdevila in *Rubén Darío, un bardo rei,* Buenos Aires, 1946, pp. 113-114, relates an incident which, I believe, was probably decisive in the change of emphasis in Darío. Briefly, in reply to the vicious attacks of Gil Guerra maintaining that Darío and the Decadents were the enemies of religion, Darío, in October of 1896, collaborated on an article about Pope Leo XIII, whom Darío esteemed above all others then. At this same time, Darío had occasion to spend an evening with Carlos Romagosa, who spoke warmly and knowingly of the venerated Bishop Esquiú. That very night Darío began his eulogy to the Bishop, later published in *El canto errante.*

Although there is a great deal of formal beauty in "Era un aire suave," "Divagación" and "Sonatina," they lack intensity and transcendence. In these earlier poems Darío does not possess the philosophical power that finds the synthesis of mystery or of life which will be observed in his later and, unfortunately, less well-known compositions. Of course, this does not mean that in 1897 there was a sudden break with the past; there is, however, a change in his scale of values. The reflective moments that are so rare in his early works predominate in the later ones. It should be understood, though, that in neither period does one entirely exclude the other.

Darío's fascination with the great divinities identified with love, beauty and art, prevalent themes in our poet, accords them a role every bit as effective as that of the lesser divinities. Their names have an evocative power that recalls an endless number of ideas, suggestions and symbolic meanings. In general, Darío intermingles the Greek and Roman names of the same deity, with an over-all preference for the Roman. In spite of the partiality toward Greek names shown by the influential Leconte de Lisle, the Roman ones were still solidly entrenched.

I *General Attributes of the Divinities*

Ambrosía (Corominas: *ambrosia* is first documented in Juan de Mena in 1438. *Autoridades*: *ambrosía* in Lope's *Circe* (1624) and Quevedo's *La fortuna con seso* (1635). In Francisco de la Torre's "Oda III" (1631). *Ambrosia* in *Don Álvaro* (1835), II.i. It is a case of an uncultured person, here the "mesonera," misunderstanding a learned word. She takes it to be the proper name Ambrosia, which follows the Latin stress, while the common noun that the student uses follows the Greek.[4] *Ambrosía* in Valera (*Romances,* p. 59), Menéndez y Pelayo (*Obras,* LXI, 116, 123) and in Gutiérrez Nájera (*Poesías,* II, 286). *Ambroisie* is common in Banville; also in Laprade's "Éleusis" and Baudelaire's "Bénédiction.")

[4] See María Rosa Lida de Malkiel, *Juan de Mena,* pp. 277-278 concerning the alternating forms *-ia* and *-ía* in Mena and his group.

Ambrosia is most often thought of as the divine food, which was supposedly nine times sweeter than honey and produced immortality. Homer mentions a less commonly known characteristic of ambrosia in the *Odyssey* 4.445-446; he states that it is an oil of incomparable odor to anoint the body, to which it gives youth and beauty. Darío refers to this aromatic quality in "Divagación" with the intention of describing the young lady's sighs:

> ¡Suspira así! Revuelen las abejas,
> al olor de la olímpica ambrosía,
> en los perfumes que en el aire dejas;

Further testimony of the sweet scent of ambrosia is given in the previously quoted passage from the *Aeneid*:

> Dixit, et avertens rosea cervice refulsit,
> Ambrosiaeque comae divinum vertice odorem
> Spiravere . . . . .

Possibly these lines are further echoed in "Mi tía Rosa" where Rosa-Venus' clothing is "aromado de sutilísimo y raro aroma, cual despidiendo una tenue bruma de luz de la sacra carne de nieve."

However, Darío's source is not so easily verified, for similar references are highly common in the poetry of his admired Banville. In "La Rose" Banville says of Venus:

> Quand nous la respirons, elle est pâmée, et s'ouvre:
> Son parfum d'ambroisie est un souffle. . . .

Moreover, in "Le festin des dieux" Banville, speaking of the gods in general, uses the phrase "leur chair d'ambroisie."

The simple notion of ambrosia as divine food appears in Banville's enthusiastic tribute to Th. Gautier. The gods are dining, with the honored guest none other than Gautier:

> Au festin de la poésie,
> Où chacun, levant son bras nu,
> Boit le nectar et l'ambroisie,
> O chanteur, sois le bienvenu!

The food of the gods serves as no commonplace reference in Darío's works. It is, on the contrary, the basis for a hyperbolic exaltation of feminine flesh in which Darío corrects Hugo:

¡Carne, celeste carne de la mujer! Arcilla
— dijo Hugo—; ambrosía más bien, ¡oh maravilla!

For Darío the contemplation of that flesh 'arcilla' is not enough; he needs communion. Thus, a few verses beyond, in a spirit that seems romantically pantheistic, he terms it "pan divino." This passage offers keen insight into Darío's erotic experience in which the flesh, not of a particular woman, but flesh in the abstract, the flesh in which man enjoys the absolute, is spiritualized in the progression from clay to ambrosia to the Eucharist. This idea of sex as a spiritual enigma is better understood if we recall that "en Darío hay una visión casi teórica del valor de la mujer como llamado de las fuerzas profundas de la vida, una especie de panerotismo que exalta la carne y la convierte en agente de la historia."[5]

Néctar (Corominas: first documented in Garcilaso (1530) and is later found in Góngora (1610). However, with information found in Dámaso Alonso's *La lengua* . . ., p. 60, we are predating Corominas' data on Góngora; it is first found in Góngora in 1582 and is one of the words that Jáuregui criticizes as overused by Góngora. *Autoridades*: in Quevedo's *La fortuna con seso*. *Néctar* is successively found in Meléndez Valdés (*Odas*, pp. 28, 68, 88), Leandro Fernández de Moratín (*Voc.*), Quintana (*Poesías*, p. 90), Valera (*Romances*, pp. 231, 273), Menéndez y Pelayo (*Obras*, LXI, 16) and Gutiérrez Nájera (*Poesías*, I, 296.) Also in Leconte de Lisle, Laprade and Banville.)

Nectar, properly speaking, the sweet, perfumed drink of the gods, was also a drink for humans before wine was known.[6] Darío passes from this latter sense of nectar's joy

[5] Rubén Darío, *Poesías*, ed. Ernesto Mejía Sánchez, México, 1952, p. xxxiv. The excellent preliminary study is by Enrique Anderson Imbert.

[6] See the *Oxford Classical Dictionary*, Oxford, 1949, p. 42.

producing effects to that of "sweetness" in general when, in "El palacio del sol" (1887), the fairy advises the sickly Berta, "Cuida de no beber tanto el néctar de la danza y de no desvanecerte en las primeras rápidas alegrías." *Néctar* has a similar force in "A Bolivia" from the *Lira póstuma*:

> En los días de azul de mi dorada infancia
> yo solía pensar en Grecia y en Bolivia;
> en Francia [sic; Grecia?] hallaba néctar que la nostalgia alivia,
> y en Bolivia encontraba una arcaica fragancia.

In "Friso" (1896) this word again appears, but merely as the sweet-smelling drink of the gods that barely competes with the sweetness of the golden-haired princess from whose lips, "licor bebía que afrentara al néctar." Darío's images involving this particular word certainly are no more inspired than Banville's. Laprade achieves somewhat more with this allusion in *Psyché*. He presents the gods as so spellbound by the beautiful song that they are oblivious to the food and drink before them:

> Tu chantes, et les dieux retenant leurs haleines
> Négligent du nectar les coupes encor pleines.

Icor (Corominas: 'the ethereal fluid which takes the place of blood in the deities' veins; first documented, as a Greek word, in 1581 in the Spanish doctor and botanist Juan Fragoso. In the *Iliad*: ". . . and blood immortal flowed from the goddess, ichor, that which runs in the veins of the blessed divinities; since these eat no food, nor do they drink of the shining wine, and therefore they have no blood and are called immortal."[7] *Icor* is in the Hermosilla translation of the *Iliad*, which seems to have been Darío's source.)

In the story "Arte y hielo" (1888) the proud sculptor, boasting of his artistry, implies the lifelike quality of his statues by referring to the ichor of the gods: "habrá en las venas de mis dioses blancos, icor, ..."

[7] Homer, *The Iliad*, trans. Richard Lattimore, Chicago, 1951, p. 137.

II   *Gods Identified With Sensuality*

Pan and his retinue. Pan was originally the Arcadian god of the hills and woods.[8] Leconte de Lisle recalls Pan in this primitive sense in the poem named after that god:

> Pan d'Arcadie, aux pieds de chèvre, au front armé
> De deux cornes, bruyant, et des pasteurs aimé,
> Emplit les verts roseaux d'une amoureuse haleine.

Pan is also the guardian of the flocks in Heredia's "Les bergers."

Like the satyrs and the sileni, Pan became part of the Dionysiac cortege; there is a resultant strong association with the amorous. Therefore, Heredia further characterizes him as the "divin chasseur de Nymphes nues" in "Pan." Leconte de Lisle accurately completes his portrayal of this god by describing his nocturnal habits:

> Pan, d'amour enflammé, dans les bois familiers
> Poursuit la vierge errante à l'ombre des halliers,
> La saisit au passage; et, transporté de joie,
> Aux clartés de la lune, il emporte sa proie.

Musical fervor and sensuality are often simultaneously linked with Pan, credited with the invention of the syrinx after an unsuccessful romantic escapade. (See *siringa*.) In "Carta del país azul" (1888) the artist proclaims his love for Pan, because, like himself, "es aficionado a la música y a los sonoros ditirambos, junto a los riachuelos armoniosos, donde triscan las náyades, la cadera sobre la linfa . . . ." Pan's eye for feminine charm echoes capriciously in "Alaba los ojos negros de Julia" (1896); Darío speaks of the dark light "que hace cantar a Pan bajo las viñas." The sensual connotation of Pan is augmented when Darío speaks of Verlaine, who, to Darío's mind, had much of Pan's sensuality mingled with his poetic genius. Thus in the "Responso a Verlaine" (1896) Darío corrects himself, "¡Panida! Pan tú mismo . . ." "You are not the

---

[8] See Gayley, *The Classic Myths*, pp. 181-185 for a discussion of Pan as a symbol of the universe and a personification of Nature.

son of Pan, but Pan himself" seems to be what Darío wishes to convey. A like idea occurs in "Pequeño poema de carnaval" (1907):

> el griego dios [Pan] no era:
> era el pobre Lelián.

The Greco-Roman figures that usually constitute an artistic paganism in *Azul* . . . and *Prosas profanas*, we have said, come to express after 1897 "el cristianismo de este divino poeta pagano."[9] Since, of course, there is no uniform development, remnants of that earlier mythological tone recur even after 1897. It is the artistic value and stimulus of the gods that Darío esteems always according to the advice he gives in "A un pintor" (1907):

> Amas la luz y la furia,
> que es un don de Pan,
> la poderosa lujuria
> que los dioses dan.[10]

The relationship between Darío's creative work and Pan as representative of the pagan world he worships is reiterated in "Pequeño poema de carnaval" where, replying to Lugones' remark on Darío's slackened literary output, Darío says:

> Sepa la Primavera
> que mi alma es compañera
> del sol que ella venera
> y del supremo Pan.

But Pan and the other divine personages give way, for the most part, to an increasing faith in Christianity, strengthening religious belief that was dormant or recessive, but not absent in Darío's youth. Darío himself admitted to his essentially Catholic background on more than one occasion. In his

---

[9] Arturo Capdevila, "Rubén Darío," *Nosotros*, XXI (1916), 288.

[10] Further statement of Darío's reasons for turning to this distant world is found in *Historia de mis libros*, where, on speaking of *Prosas profanas*, Darío says, ". . . abominando la democracia, funesta a los poetas, así sean sus adoradores como Walt Whitman, tendí hacia el pasado, a las antiguas mitologías y a las espléndidas historias, incurriendo en las censuras de los miopes." The reader undoubtedly recalls similar statements quoted in the first chapter.

117

commentary on *Cantos de vida y esperanza* in *Historia de mis libros* he says: "La historia de una juventud llena de tristezas y de desilusión, a pesar de las primaverales sonrisas; . . . la sagrada y terrible fiebre de la lira, el culto del entusiasmo y de la sinceridad, contra las añagazas y traiciones del mundo, del demonio y de la carne; . . . la simiente del catolicismo contrapuesta a un tempestuoso instinto pagano . . . ."[11] The word "simiente" is significantly appropriate for his Catholicism, which grew and matured over a period of time. So it is that in "Palimpsesto II" (1908) the satyr vainly searches for his former comrade Pan: "Hemos clamado a los cuatro vientos llamando a Pan, y apenas el eco ha respondido a nuestra voz." Other references to Pan, studied below, solidify this development in Darío's mythology.

Bicorne (DRAE, 1956: <L. *bicornis* = bis 'two' and cornu 'horn.' Dámaso Alonso, *La lengua* . . ., p. 77, documents *bicorne,* a word censured by Lope, in Góngora prior to the *Soledad primera.* Marasso, p. 403: in Baltasar Vitoria's *Teatro de los dioses,* in the *Tragedias de Esquilo* of the "Biblioteca Clásica" and in Menéndez y Pelayo's translation *Canto secular de Horacio.* Marasso also refers to a satirical paper against Ruiz de Alarcón in which *bicorne* is listed among the words neither known nor heard in Spanish. *Bicornio* appears in Blasco Ibáñez and *bicornudo* in Martí.[12] Moreover, Darío surely knew Mallarmé's "L'après-midi d'un faune" (1876) in which the carnal faun speaks of the "cornes de mon front." Earlier, in *Poèmes antiques,* Leconte de Lisle presented Pan with "deux cornes" in the poem entitled "Pan." Darío had also seen Pan

[11] In *La caravana pasa*: "Yo, como todos los que amamos la verdad, he estado durante años esperando el santo advenimiento de esa fe tan deseada, y después de muchos estudios he llegado a conseguir aquella voz del alma que Dios concede a los que buscan sinceramente."

[12] Miguel de Toro y Gisbert, *Los nuevos derroteros del idioma,* Paris, 1918, p. 10, says this word should be in the Academy's dictionary. On p. 16 he adds that *bicornio* appears in Pedro de Répide. Moreover, Toro y Gisbert includes it in a list of words "perfectamente españolas." *Bicornudo* is a neologism in Martí, according to Dr. Alan M. Gordon who passed this information on to me from research done for his unpublished thesis (Harvard, 1956) *Verb Function in the Works of José Martí: Method and Function.*

portrayed with two horns in the plastic arts and in Ménard's book, figs. 458-461.)

With Darío this adjective is suggestive of sensuality in Pan, the horned satyr, and other creatures. In the "Responso a Verlaine" Darío expresses the fantastic wish "que el fúnebre recinto [of the sensual Verlaine] visite Pan bicorne." *Bicorne* is again associated with a creature of sensuality that describes Darío's unsatisfied amorous desire in "Por el influjo de la primavera" (1905):

> Sobre el jarrón de cristal
> hay flores nuevas. Anoche
> hubo una lluvia de besos.
> Despertó un fauno bicorne
> tras un alma sensitiva.

In the "Coloquio de los centauros" Darío extends his usage of this word; he applies *bicorne* to the bull for whom a bestial love was inspired in Pasiphaë, "con la bicorne bestia Pasifae se ayunta" (*OPC,* 634).

Bifronte. Darío uses this similar morphological form in "Divagación" (1896) to describe the two-faced Janus, god of war. Pleasure and poetry reign in France, not war:

> En París reinan el Amor y el Genio.
> Ha perdido su imperio el dios bifronte.

Flauta (Corominas: of uncertain origin, perhaps from the language of Oc. *Autoridades*: found in Spanish since Fray Luis de Granada's *Símbolo de la fe* (1582); also in Solís' *Historia de la Nueva España.* Later in Meléndez Valdés (*Odas* p. 231), Moratín (*Voc.*), Valera (*Obras,* XII, 51, 56, 67, 76) and in Menéndez y Pelayo (*Obras,* LXII, 116). The flute is a common attribute of Pan and other divinities in many of Darío's French models; for example, in Leconte de Lisle, Mallarmé's "L'après-midi d'un faune," Heredia and in Verlaine's *Les uns et les autres.*)

Heredia utilizes this word in a purely traditional manner. In his poem "La flûte" he gives us a matter-of-fact account of its invention, with Pan narrating:

> Ma flûte, faite avec sept tiges de ciguë
> Inégales que joint un peu de cire, aiguë
> Ou grave, pleure, chante ou gémit à mon gré.

The flute as an attribute of Pan and, by extension, of the satyrs figures in Darío's "El sátiro sordo." The gods advise the satyr, "persigue ninfas y suena tu flauta." In Leconte de Lisle's "Paysage" it is another satyr, here called "Aigipan," that is identified with the flute. The whole image is charged with sensuality and is reminiscent of numerous other stylized evocations of the lesser divinities already quoted from many of Darío's French models:

> Laissant pendre sa flûte au bout de son bras nu,
> L'Aigipan, renversé sur le rameau qui ploie,
> Rêve, les yeux mi-clos, avec un air de joie,
> Qu'il surprend l'Oréade en son antre inconnu.

In "Propósito primaveral" (1905) the charm exercised by the flute is attributed to the triumph of love:

> Amor, tu hoz de oro ha segado mi trigo;
> por ti me halaga el suave son de la flauta griega,

In "La leyenda de San Martín" (1897) the Christian value of the lyre outweighs the pagan connotation of the flute. The latter appears essentially pagan in the words of San Martín's mother, who speaks of "las flautas que han de resonar mañana." There is seemingly a schism between paganism and Christianity, for the story continues that he merely smiles because "oye otra voz que viene de una lira invisible y angélica." It is an implied triumph of and an apparently necessary separation or conflict of the two. However, the antagonism between spirit and flesh, of which Charles Morice speaks in his study on Verlaine, has momentarily disappeared in the Darío of "Palabras de la satiresa" (1896):

> y amando a Pan y Apolo en la lira y la flauta,
> ser en la flauta Pan como Apolo en la lira.

In this poem Darío says that there is "la conjunción de las exaltaciones pánica y apolínea — que ya Moréas, según lo hace

saber un censor más listo, había preconizado, ¡y tanto mejor!"[13]
Darío refers to a line from Le pèlerin passionné: "Apollon sur
la lyre et Pan dans les pipeaux." The two contrary elements
have united, and Darío's dual state of soul, often likened to
Verlaine's, has seen that it is not impossible to be Pan on the
flute and Apollo on the lyre. The secret is "en unir carne y
alma a la esfera que gira." Thus in "Flora" (1901) the reference to the flute is saturated with a pantheism that recalls
Hugo's "Le satyre." In Darío:

> Así llena de música la selva melancólica,
> traduce por el son de la flauta bucólica
> lo que arde, lo que aspira, lo que ama, lo que besa.

Marasso, who sees this wandering "entre la catedral y las
ruinas paganas" as a parallel of body and soul, lyre and flute
or Apollo and Pan, compares Darío's "Alexandrian" soul to
that of L. Ménard, who says "El templo ideal donde van mis
plegarias encierra todos los dioses que el mundo ha cono-
cido."[14] The opinion here offered is that it is not a question of
opposition between art and religion in Darío's alternating
tones of mythology; in reality the Christian and the Hellenic
are two aspects of one truth. From about 1897 on there is a
leveling of Christian and pagan figures whereby Rome comes
to signify both as in "Palimpsesto II" (1908): "He aquí que
la siringa, la flauta pagana, crecerá y aparecerá más tarde en
los tubos de los órganos de las basílicas, por premio al sátiro
que buscó a Dios."[15]

In Darío's youthful years the flute and the nymph
were the *summum bonum* of his quest for beauty; the flesh

---

[13] Quoted by Marasso, *op. cit.*, p. 156.

[14] Marasso, p. 390. Compare Darío's "Hay soles de eternos días, / Olimpo y
Sión."

[15] Compare the parallels, by no means original, which Darío draws between
paganism and Christianity. In *Opiniones* (1906) there is a statement concerning
Pope Leo XIII: "Bien sentiría el ambiente de paganismo que en la basílica de
las basílicas dejaron tantos antecesores suyos que alegraron la tristeza católica
con la resurrección de griegos esplendores, y colocaron la concha sobre que se
posaron los pies de la Anadiomena como pila de agua bendita." *Obras completas,*
X, 42.

was to be the means of fulfilling himself. However, with the more mature realization that "la carne es cosa triste," Darío, like the satyr above, must recognize the existence of a higher Truth if he is to find a completely satisfying Beauty. Darío's journey is somewhat like the Augustinian "descent before ascent" with his progression from "arcilla" to "ambrosía" to "pan divino." Indeed, Darío never adopts the Decadents' perverse attitude towards the flesh; for Darío, feminine flesh has something of the spiritual.

Pánico (Corominas: 'the terror caused by Pan to whom were attributed the noises of unknown origin heard in mountains and valleys'; *pánico* is first documented, as a noun, in Gracián's *Criticón*. In one of Valera's notes on *Dafnis y Cloe* I find that *pánico* is also used as an adjective: "Aun se conserva en nuestros idiomas modernos el epíteto de *pánico,* dado al terror cuando es muy grande."[16] "Les temps paniques" in Hugo's *La légende des siècles*. Plowert, *Glossaire*: *panique* in Verlaine. Analogous morphological forms cited by Plowert are *adamique* in Verlaine and *édénique* in Jules Laforgue. In Darío we also find *titánico, pandórico, talismánico* and *fáunico*.)

Darío uses *pánico* both as an adjective and a noun. This word is an adjective in "el alfabeto pánico" from "A Roosevelt" and in "y mis viejas siringas con su pánico estruendo" from the "Epístola a la señora de Leopoldo Lugones," where the use of *pánico* is semihumorous. It is a noun in "estoy lleno de pánico" from "Pequeño poema de carnaval." As for the meaning of this word in Darío, Marasso claims that Darío does not employ *pánico* in the puristic sense defined by Corominas above.[17] Marasso says that in Darío it means only "pertaining to Pan." However, the usage in "estoy lleno de pánico" disproves Marasso.

[16] Valera, *Obras,* XII, 160. Albert Henry in *Langage et poésie chez Paul Valéry,* Paris, 1952, p. 147, gives data that is interesting from our present point of view. Valéry uses the adjective *panique* 'cosmique (participant suprêmement à la grande vie universelle) et inspirant une confuse angoisse' in *Amphion*.

[17] See Manuel de Saralegui, "Escarceos filológicos," *Boletín de la Real Academia Española,* XI (1924), 70-75, for a discussion of the puristic usage.

There is another adjective of similar formation in "Salutación del optimista" (1905) where we also note *talismánico*. Here Darío prophesies a new era in an obvious reference to the well-known myth of Pandora as the dispenser of evil. She kept but one thing in her box, Hope:

> y en la caja pandórica de que tantas desgracias surgieron
> encontramos de súbito, talismánica, pura, riente,
> cual pudiera decirla en sus versos Virgilio divino,
> la divina reina de luz, ¡la celeste Esperanza!

The only freshness to these verses is lent by *pandórica* 'pertaining to Pandora,' apparently a creation of Darío's as is *fáunico*, discussed below.

Faunus. In Darío reference to Faunus, the Italic divinity who became identified with Pan, is further example of an original poetic vocabulary. *Fáunico* 'pertaining to Faunus,' connotes sensuality in "Sirenas y tritones" from *Cuentos y crónicas.* Describing a siren Darío says, "La faz medrosa mira hacia un punto en que algo se divisa, y casi no atiende la hembra al tritón fáunico, que la atrae, invitándola a una cita sexual, tal como en la tierra, al amor del gran bosque, lo haría Pan con Siringa."

Faunalias (< L. *faunalias* 'festivals in honor of Faunus.') In a note of warning in "A Francia" (1907) *faunalias* contrasts in tone with the threat implied in "el viento que arrecia del lado del férreo Berlín." Darío uses the word in a metaphorical sense meaning the wild, carefree gaiety of Paris.

Silvano. Closely identified with Pan and Faunus is Sylvanus, as are the previously discussed *silvanos.* The assimilation of Sylvanus' personality to Pan's implies likeness of characteristics, sensuality and a fondness for music. Therefore, in "La Dea" (1896) a captivating nymph comes in search of the "lírico Silvano." This intimation of worldly pleasures emphasizes the virtue of the central figure of the portrait, Pallas Athena. Darío's presentation of the festival of Sylvanus in the forest is most likely a recollection of figure 191 in Ménard's book.

Baco and *Dionisio.* Menéndez y Pelayo brought the dionysiac cult to the Spanish language in 1879 with his "Himno a Dionysos," inspired in Euripides' *Bacchae.*[18] Darío's descriptions of the dionysiac cortege are more plastic than Menéndez y Pelayo's, for Darío had at his fingertips the whole network of elaborate references associated with these figures which he saw portrayed in the plastic arts and in Ménard. Moreover, among some of Darío's favored French authors there was a good bit of interest in Dionysus and his attendants. Darío's presentation of this divinity shows no influence of Nietzsche, whose *Birth of Tragedy* was widely discussed in the last part of the nineteenth century.

Darío's allusions to the Roman Bacchus are of slight poetic force, unlike those involving his companions, the bacchantes and maenads. Bacchus is most commonly portrayed as an object of art; in "Arte y hielo" (1888) we have, along with a "pie de ninfa" in the sculptor's workshop, a fragmented, depersonalized view of Bacchus: "la barriga de un Baco." In a scene on an amphora in "Respecto a Horacio" (1893) Bacchus appears in quite a stylized manner, identified with the vine: "Alrededor de la panza tiene figurada una viña copiosa; bajo la viña el gran Baco en su florida juventud y rodeado de ménades y de tigres." In this portrayal there is also a note of the merrymaking associated with Bacchus, but in the "Epístola" from *El canto errante* there is a purely trite allusion to him as the god of wine:

> Hay no lejos de aquí un archiduque austriaco
> que las pomas de Ceres y las uvas de Baco
> cultiva, en un retiro archiducal y egregio.

In "Pórtico" (1896) Bacchus appears as in an Orphic initiation. The Muse

> Tiene por templo un alcázar marmóreo,
> guárdalo esfinge de rostro egipciaco,
> y cual labrada en un bosque hiperbóreo,
> Venus enfrente de un triunfo de Baco.

[18] See Marasso, *op. cit.,* pp. 44-45.

It is under the older name Dionysus and figures originally associated with him that the god of wine appears most strongly in the character and surroundings of joy and triumph. Orpheus, in a futile attempt to charm the insensitive satyr of "El sátiro sordo," invokes all the mythological figures identified with sensuality, ranging from Aphrodite and the centaurs to the "copa de Dionisio." The last reference suggests a Bacchic revelry by the indirect allusion to wine.[19] The excessive, decadent exuberance that characterized feasts in honor of Dionysus is recalled in "Friso" in a manner similar to the animated description of ancient scenes that Pierre Louÿs, for one, sought to re-create. The details and general tone of Darío's Dionysiac procession show a strong influence of Ménard's description of this god, especially Theban Bacchus:

Lírica procesión al viento esparce
los cánticos rituales de Dionisio,
el *evohé* de las triunfales fiestas,
la algazara que enciende con su risa
la impúber tropa de saltantes niños,
y el vivo son de músicas sonoras.

Mendès, in his play *Bacchus,* frequently presents the god of wine as the triumphant hero surrounded by his worshiping coterie. This work emerges as an important influence on Darío's treatment of Bacchus and, above all, his attendants, the maenads and bacchantes. The conquering, Oriental Bacchus is prominent in Banville's "Le triomphe de Bacchos" from *Les stalactites* as well as in "L'exil des dieux" from *Les exilés.* Banville favors the Greek name for the most part; there is an occasional *Bacchos* as in "La cithare."

For Darío, Dionysus, like others, come to mean much more than that which is told in the mythological tales. All the Dionysiac lusts are rejected in "La leyenda de San Martín" (1897): "Nada para él de Dionisio; nada de Venus. Y en aquella carne de firme bronce está incrustada la margarita de la castidad."

---

[19] Dionysus' cup also has a "signification mystique" according to Creuzer. See René Ménard, *op. cit.,* p. 527.

Dionisíaco (Corominas: first documented in Huerta's translation of Pliny (1629). Later found in Menéndez y Pelayo's translation of Anacreon "La rosa." *Dionysiaque* in A. Ferdinand Hérold's "Le cortège de Dionysos" and commonly in Mendès's *Bacchus.*)

This adjective appears in Darío's story "La canción del oro" (1888). It is similar to "Pórtico" in its description of Dionysiac festivals: "Cantemos el oro . . . en la copa del festín dionisíaco."

Ditirambos (Corominas: originally, 'poetic composition in honor of Bacchus'; first documented in Jáuregui (1624). This word is also found in Moratín (*Voc.*), Valera (*Obras*, XII, 168) and in Menéndez y Pelayo's "Epístola a Horacio.")

Darío uses *ditirambos* primarily in sarcastically humorous commentaries on certain aspects of contemporary life. The absurd "rey burgués" favored "a sus hacedores de ditirambos." Darío also employs other rhetorical technicisms in this story to characterize the sterility of the previous poetic school; consider, for example, "anapestos" and "pirriquios." The business-man is prodded at in "Historia de un sobretodo" (1892): "Yo veo y examino con fruición incomparable su tela gruesa y fina . . . al son de los ditirambos que el vendedor repite . . . ." Only in "Carta del país azul" (1888) does *ditirambos* retain its original flavor of orgiastic hymns: "Amo a Pan porque, como yo, es aficionado a la música y a los sonoros ditirambos."

Bacante (Dámaso Alonso, *La lengua* . . ., p. 51: in Góngora's *Soledad primera*. Later found in Moratín (*Voc.*), Mesonero Romanos (*DE*), Valera (*Obras*, XII, 62, 119) and in Menéndez y Pelayo's "Epístola a Horacio." *Bacchante* is commonly found in Darío's French models; in Gautier's "Bûchers et tombeaux," Leconte de Lisle, Flaubert's *La tentation de Saint-Antoine*, Banville, Silvestre and in Mendès's *Bacchus.*)

The bacchantes illustrate that Dionysus' worship was centered about two widely separated ideas: freedom and ecstatic joy as well as savage brutality. The god of wine could give either to his followers. The bacchante, mad with wine, is most commonly thought of as racing through the woods, shouting and brandishing her wand, completely swept away in a consuming ecstasy. Not even the wild beasts could stop her. The bacchantes tore them to pieces and devoured them in a bloody feast, singing madly all the time. Since the gods of the Olympus loved order and beauty in their sacrifices and temples, the bacchantes had no temples of their own. Therefore, they returned to the purity of the untrodden hills and mountains for their rituals. They slept under leafy trees and depended upon Dionysus for their food. There was much desirable in this worship under the clear sky and in the ecstasy it brought; yet, the reality of the bloody feast was always present. Leconte de Lisle plainly states the inhuman aspect of the bacchantes in "Kybèle:"

> O Silène de Nyse, ô Bacchante inhumaine,
> Agitez en hurlant, ivres, tumultueux,
> Les thyrses enlacés de serpents tortueux!

The furor and intoxication that became associated with these priestesses functions effectively in Darío's prose and poetry. In "El sátiro sordo" Orpheus' genius and the satyr's impassibility are simultaneously underlined. Although the satyr is unmoved by Orpheus' playing, the music's charm is such that even "Las bacantes más furiosas habían callado y le oían como en un sueño." The adjective *furiosas* epitomizes the fervor of the bacchantes as does *ardientes*. The same is true of *encendidas,* which occurs in a plastic image: "A su vista, para distraerle, [al sátiro] danzaban coros de bacantes encendidas en su fiebre loca . . . ." Equally plastic and suggestive of base fervor is "el coro de bacantes ebrias" in "Friso." Banville also recalls these frenzied rituals in "Pour Mademoiselle" from *Les stalactites*:

> Amours des bas-reliefs, ô Nymphes et Bacchantes,
> Qui, sur l'Ida nocturne, au bruit d'un tambourin,
> Les fronts échevelés en tresses provocantes,
> Dansiez en agitant vos crotales d'airain!

Similar descriptions abound in Mendès's *Bacchus.*

In "Por el influjo de la primavera" the sensuality implied is that of a bacchante that has passed from Greece to France, for imagine

> un buen egipán latino
> con una bacante griega
> y parisiense . . .

No less captivated by the charms of the bacchante is Silvestre. In discussing Mademoiselle Itasse's *Bacchante* in *La sculpture aux salons de 1896,* he describes the bacchante as the symbol of beauty and voluptuousness, chanting her praises in a series of stanzas that begin with a "Te Deam laudamus."

The bacchantes are also referred to as *ménades.* (*Ménade* in Quintana (*Poesías,* p. 208), Valera (*Obras,* XII, 119) and in Menéndez y Pelayo (*Obras,* LXII, 112.) Also in Laprade's "La coupe," Flaubert's *La tentation de Saint-Antoine,* Mendès and Banville.)

In "Friso" Darío presents the maenads in a traditional way: "las ménades ardientes." His models present them in an equally stylized fashion as the wild priestesses of Dionysus. In Banville's "Le triomphe de Bacchos" they are part of his retinue: "Le choeur furieux de Bacchides et les Ménades." In Mendès's *Bacchus* they are frequently grouped with "Bassarides" and "Corybantes" in an atmosphere that seethes with frenzied enthusiasm.

Ninfalia (Created by Darío by analogy with *faunalias* $<$ L. *faunalia* 'celebration in honor of Faunus.' Hence, a *ninfalia* is a bacchanal. The word *bacanales* is found in Góngora according to *La lengua . . .,* p. 51. *Bacchanale* in Banville's "La chanson du vin." Heredia wrote a poem called "Bacchanale.")

Ninfalias has, in Darío, none of the debauchery attached to the bacchantes. The *ninfalias* are part of the eternal feminine charm Darío salutes in the plastic verses of "Divagación:"

> Y el dios de piedra [Dionisio] se despierte y cante
> la gloria de los tirsos florecientes
> en el gesto ritual de la bacante
> de rojos labios y nevados dientes.

En el gesto ritual que en las hermosas
Ninfalias guía a la divina hoguera,
hoguera que hace llamear las rosas
en las manchadas pieles de pantera.

This scene, which is very much like the portrayal of the Spring-
time resurrection of Dionysus on a vase shown in Ménard, is
further evidence of Menéndez y Pelayo's influence on the
Dionysiac aspect of Darío's Hellenism. In Menéndez y Pelayo's
"Himno a Dionysos" we find:

Ya resuena la mística orgía
La bacante su peplo desciñe
Y ya el báquico tirso empuñó
Cubre piel de pantera su espalda
Coronemos de rosas la frente.

Júpiter. The Roman Jove or Jupiter is prevalent in Darío's
works. As we would expect, Leconte de Lisle consistently
refers to the Olympian ruler as Zeus. That Laprade, for the
most part, prefers the Greek appellation of this god is apparent
throughout his *Odes et poëmes;* he does, however, occasionally
speak of Jupiter in *Psyché.* Elsewhere, the Roman names seem
to be widely used, though not to the complete exclusion of
the Greek.

Jupiter is bowed to as the powerful master of the
Olympus in a lyric exaltation of life and the senses in "Carta
del país azul" (1888): "Sí, soy pagano. Adorador de los
viejos dioses, y ciudadano de los viejos tiempos. Yo me inclino
ante Júpiter porque tiene el rayo y el águila." (The only power
above Jupiter's bolt is incarnate in the person of Venus, as
we shall see shortly.) But in "Cisne IV" from *Cantos de vida
y esperanza* there is a mingling in the imagery of Jupiter as
both the philandering husband of Juno and the mighty ruler:
Addressing Leda, Darío marvels that

Tu dulce vientre cubrió de seda
el Dios . . .

Darío and many others before him were fascinated with the
story of Leda and the swan. It could well have been precisely
this incident that Darío had in mind in "El sátiro sordo" when

he placed Jupiter at the head of the list of mythological beings known for their sensuality: "Cantó del gran Jove, de Eros y de Afrodita, de los centauros gallardos y de las bacantes ardientes."

Jupiter, too, undergoes a transformation towards 1897. In "La fiesta de Roma" (1898) the name is Jupiter, but the meaning is Christ. The pagan Lucius Varus, speaking of the glory of Rome, the last of his goddesses, says, "Es la diosa dueña de la inmortalidad y de la victoria, favorecida directamente del Divus Pater Júpiter, que le ha hecho el don de su voluntad y de su rayo . . . . Roma es y será invencible al Tiempo." In this same story Darío inserts some verses which also appear in prose in chapter iii of *El hombre de oro;* Christ supplants Jove:

> Del soberbio Imperator resplandece la altiva diadema
> Y su mano, al alzarse, cual la de Jove rige
> Capitolina . . .

The temptation to quote Gautier's "Bûchers et tombeaux" is understandably irresistible:

> Mais l'Olympe cède au Calvaire,
> Jupiter au Nazaréen;

There can be no doubt about the new Truth. In "Palimpsesto II" (1908) the satyr corrects the centaur who assumed that the divine old man he saw was Jupiter: "El anciano que tú has visto no era Júpiter, no es ningún ser olímpico. Es un enviado del Dios nuevo." This person was St. Anthony.

Cisne (Corominas: *cisne* is first documented in the thirteenth century, *Biblia escurialense.* The theme of the swan came from Greece and is inexhaustible in Hellenism, Horace, the Middle Ages and heraldry. It was renewed with vigor in the Renaissance, especially through Leonardo's drawings; it is present in the symbolists primarily because of Wagner. *Cisne* in Meléndez Valdés (*Odas,* p. 4), Moratín (*Voc.*), Quintana (*Poesías,* p. 100), Valera (*Romances,* p. 170) and in Menéndez y Pelayo (*Obras,* LXI, 161.) Also in Gautier,

Laprade, Banville, Silvestre, Sully Prudhomme, Mallarmé, Mendès's *Bacchus,* Samain's "Hélène" and in Richepin.)

Undoubtedly the swan would never have attained its lofty position in art and literature if it had not been for Leda, who was charming enough to cause Jupiter to contrive one of his elaborate plans. From that celebrated union, in which Jupiter took the form of a swan, resulted Helen, an event retold by Darío and many of his models. In "Hélène" (1852) Leconte de Lisle marvels, "Et l'amante du Cygne est la mère d'Hélène." Laprade had earlier recalled that episode as Vielé-Griffin so often does in *Les cygnes.* In Laprade's "Éleusis" (1844):

> Cygne voluptueux par Léda caressé,
> L'aile ouverte et le col dans ses bras enlacé,
> De deux guerriers jumeaux il rend Sparte féconde
> Par ce même baiser qui donne Hélène au monde.

Banville gives his account of that moment in "Une femme de Rubens:"

> C'est Léda qui s'indigne
> Sous le baiser du cygne
> Et le cherche à son tour
> > Folle d'amour;

And in "La source" Banville portrays Leda "Pâle d'horreur" in an image filled with sensual detail.

Richepin offers a simple explanation of Helen's renowned beauty in *Grandes amoureuses.* For the most part, her charms are the understandable result of her distinguished parentage:

> Hélène la belle était fille d'un dieu. Sa mère . . .
> était Léda; et son père fut ce fameux Cygne de
> l'Eurotas qui n'était autre que Jupiter
> métamorphosé. Il ne fallait pas moins qu'un
> tel amour et qu'une telle origine pour expliquer
> la merveilleuse beauté de cette femme.

In a sensual appraisal of Desbois's *Leda* Silvestre says:

> Et c'est ainsi que Jupiter, las du caprice des
> anciennes métamorphoses a revêtu la forme du cygne

vainqueur qui vaincra, par l'attrait de la nouveauté
et par quelque curiosité inquiète, l'indifférence
de la belle rêveuse. (*La sculpture aux salons de 1896*)

In "Friso" the swan is considered the height of good fortune for having seen Leda's whiteness:

fuí más feliz que el luminoso cisne
que vió de Leda la inmortal blancura.

However, the apotheosis of the swan is found in *Cantos de vida y esperanza*. In "Cisne IV" Darío exalts the union between woman and beast, "¡Antes de todo, gloria a ti, Leda!" The act is classified as celestial and supreme in importance, marking a new era in the world, for on witnessing it, "dioses y bestias hicieron pacto." Darío implies that by example of Leda and the swan, the animal and the divine elements seek each other. The dignity and worth of the swan are explained by its brief contact with Leda, an idea that is somewhat reminiscent of Richepin's. But from this fleeting union that Darío marvels at is derived a certain melancholy sentiment, a sadness and longing for that wonderfully unexpected and too brief moment.

The key to Darío's interpretation of the swan is found in the third poem of this group:

Por un momento, ¡oh Cisne!, juntaré mis anhelos
a los de tus dos alas que abrazaron a Leda,

.   .   .   .

Cisne, tendré tus alas blancas por un instante,
y el corazón de rosa que hay en tu dulce pecho
palpitará en el mío con su sangre constante.

This myth takes on an immensely personal meaning; Darío identifies his own romantic hopes and longings with those of the swan. There is a desire to fuse with the swan, for then, "Amor será dichoso." In the swan Darío sees the means of materially gaining possession of beauty.[20]

---

[20] Salinas, *op. cit.*, pp. 94-101 discusses the swan as a symbol of the new poetry. Max Henríquez Ureña, *Breve historia*, pp. 20-23 summarizes the diffusion of the swan motif and also mentions the role of the black swan.

The swan does not even begin to approach such depth of expression in any of Darío's models. They are, for the most part, enthralled with its whiteness and its plastic value. Pierre Louÿs hails the luminous quality of the swan in his story "Léda." In "L'après-midi d'un faune" Mallarmé acclaims the naiads' whiteness by first mistaking them for swans. Sully Prudhomme, in "Le cygne," creates a scene that is like a watercolor in verse; in the midst of it stands the swan, white and elegant. Banville often uses the figure of the swan as a basis for a comparison or eulogy. There is, for example, "Tu naquis plus blanche qu'un cygne . . ." in "La vendangeuse" and "Son jeune sein, plus blanc que la plume des cygnes" in "Le cher fantôme."

Their pictorial quality is widely appreciated. Gautier creates a delicately plastic scene in "Fantaisies d'hiver:"

> Dans le bassin des Tuileries,
> Le cygne s'est pris en nageant,
> Et les arbres, comme aux féeries,
> Sont en filigrane d'argent.

In Banville's "Les tourterelles" there are "deux cygnes d'un lac bleu"; in *Psyché* Laprade paints "Deux cygnes amoureux balancés sur les eaux." But all the beauty and grace of the hitherto regal swan is disturbed by an antagonistic element in Banville's "Les torts du cygne." He is nothing but a buffoon and a "vilain oiseau" to the riled crows:

> Comme le Cygne allait nageant
> Sur le lac au miroir d'argent,
> Plein de fraîcheur et de silence,
> Les Corbeaux noirs, d'un ton guerrier,
> Se mirent à l'injurier
> En volant avec turbulence.

As far as the black crows are concerned, his whiteness is no more beautiful than that of a marble tombstone; with few words they strike at the swan's point of pride: "Barbouillé de lys et de neige." Banville here distinguishes himself by the freshness of his imagery.

Darío is also intrigued by the whiteness and plasticity of the swan. In "Palimpsesto" (1896) the swans, however, take second place to Diana: "Tanta blancura, que al cisne injuria." The swans are no more successful in "Historia prodigiosa de la princesa Psiquia;" she "superaba en blancura . . . a los más ilustres cisnes." The swan, with the exception of Venus, is the most significant and striking of the various mythological figures Darío treats. In whatever capacity he invokes the swan, it contributes admirably to the charm and pictorial quality so characteristic of his use of mythology.

Toro (Corominas: in Berceo.) Celebrated in Renaissance art, this myth has also inspired modern writers. In "Héraklès au Taureau" Leconte de Lisle dwells on the force of Hercules against the bull, not on the plastic presentation of Jupiter-Bull and Europa. In this poem Jupiter's trickery is secondary: "Nageait dans la mer glauque avec Europe en pleurs." Not so, however, in his "Fultus Hyacintho" where he is much more interpretative:

> Tel que Zeus, sur les mers portant la vierge Europe,
> Une blancheur sans tache en entier l'enveloppe,
> Sa corne est fine, aux bouts recourbés et polis,
> Ses fanons florissants abondent à grands plis,
> Une écume d'argent tombe à flots de sa bouche,
> Et de longs poils épars couvrent son oeil farouche.

Laprade, too, is concerned with Zeus' abduction of Europa in "Éleusis:"

> Là, taureau, sur sa croupe il porte en des flots bleus,
> Vers un monde à peupler dont elle sera mère,
> Europe aux pieds d'argent que baise l'onde amère.

In "Retrato de Watteau" (1887) Europa being carried off by the bull is one of the adornments in the lady's boudoir. Europa is surrounded by a marine cortege of dolphins and tritons "sobre el lomo de un toro robusto y divino." The plasticity of this scene is surpassed only by "Marina" (1905) where the bull appears "magnífico y sonoro" amidst the frothy foam that recalls somewhat the scene in "Fultus Hyacintho." In "Marina:"

> velas purpúreas de bajeles
> que saludaron el mugir del toro
> celeste, con Europa sobre el lomo
> que salpicaba la revuelta espuma.

In both of these descriptions, as well as the following, Darío specifically refers to the divine nature of the Bull. As in the case of the swan, the bestial aspect of the episode is diminished or ennobled by the incarnation of the God in the Bull. In the sonnet "Caracol" the wonderment of Triton's shell is magnified because

> Europa lo ha tocado con sus manos divinas
> cuando cruzó las ondas sobre el celeste toro.

In "Palimpsesto" (1896) the abduction of one of the nymphs is likened to Europa's fate:

> ninfa que a la alta diosa acompaña,
> saca de la onda donde se baña;
> la grupa vuelve, raudo galopa;
> tal iba el toro raptor de Europa
> con el orgullo de su conquista.

All of these references clearly indicate that Darío was indebted to the plastic arts. Marasso points out an additional likely source, Moschus' "Idyll II," which is translated in Ménard. However, this explanation does not take into account that Darío could have seen this in the translation found in *Poetas bucólicos griegos,* which we know Darío must have read by 1886.

Eros. Cupid, the Roman equivalent of the Greek god of love, is not common in Darío. In his models both forms are found, with no conspicuous partiality for one or the other. Meléndez Valdés speaks of *Amor* and *Cupido* in "De mis cantares." Menéndez y Pelayo, however, is more inclined towards the Greek designation; such is the case in "Epístola a Horacio" and "Sáficas I." Leconte de Lisle, of course, uses the Greek name and Banville in general shows a similar preference. Elsewhere, such as in Gautier's *Émaux et camées,* the Roman name is at least as common as the Greek.

Although Homer does not speak of the god of love, Hesiod considers him "Fairest of the deathless gods."[21] Cupid's physical attractiveness stands out in Gautier's "Contralto." Cupid is as desirable to woman as Venus is to man:

> Tout homme dit: C'est Aphrodite!
> Toute femme: C'est Cupidon!

These lines, part of Gautier's praise of a lovely lady, are typical of the way in which he, and many of Darío's other models, use the salient characteristic of a deity as the basis for an obvious comparison or eulogy. Darío at times uses the same technique; however, we have seen on numerous occasions that he goes far beyond these traditional and often hackneyed images.

Eros, commonly portrayed in art with a quiver of arrows that cause the wound of love, is poetically presented in this role in "Loor" (1896):

> Por los boscosos senderos
> viene Eros
> a causar la dulce herida.

In quite a contrasting attitude to Darío's "dulce herida" is Leconte de Lisle's exclamation in "Hélène:" "O cruelle Aphrodite, et toi, cruel Eros!" There is a purely capricious evocation of Eros in Darío's humorous defense of dark-eyed beauty in "Alaba los ojos negros de Julia:"

> Venus tuvo el azur en sus pupilas;
> pero su hijo, no. Negros y fieros,
> encienden a las tórtolas tranquilas
> los dos ojos de Eros.

That none can escape Eros's arrows is implicit in Eulalia's confident laughter; her lovers' complaints do not bother her, "pues son su tesoro las flechas de Eros" (*OPC*, 604). Darío shows resentment in his later years toward the one who promised so much that was never realized. This feeling is registered in "Eco y yo" (1907):

21 Edith Hamilton, *Mythology*, New York, 1959, p. 36.

Guióme por varios senderos
Eros,
mas no se portó tan bien
en
esquivarme los risueños
sueños,
que hubieran dado a mi vida
ida,
menos crueles mordeduras
duras.

The one reference to the Roman counterpart of Eros in the works of Darío studied is found in "Estival:" "carro de Cupido."

III Goddesses Associated With Love and Beauty

Venus. Of all the deities Darío portrays, none appears with such a variety of names. Not only is she the Greek *Afrodita,* but she is also *Anadiómena,* which alludes to the legend of her rising out of the sea at birth.[22] Darío also calls her *Cipris* and *Citera,* referring to Cyprus and Cythera where she was most venerated. (These, in fact, are the names Homer commonly employs.) Once in "Divagación" she is the *Hetaíra* who searches for the same desirable Adonis that shuns her in "Primaveral," but most commonly she is the Roman Venus. The various names of Venus occur abundantly among the writers influential on Darío. In Meléndez Valdés's "Oda I" and "Los besos de amor" she is Venus. In Valera's "Velada de Venus" she appears both as *Ciprina* and *Venus;* in the "Fábula de Euforión" she is both *Venus* and *Chiprina bella.* The latter is another instance of the etymological spelling that was revived by Menéndez y Pelayo, who himself speaks of *Venus Urania* and *Afrodita* in the "Epístola a Horacio" and *Afrodita Cipria* in "Sáficas I."

With respect to richness and variety of names, Darío surpasses most of his models. Leconte de Lisle and Banville

[22] See Delfín Donadíu y Puignan, *Novísimo diccionario,* I, 194.

are the most notable exceptions. In Banville's "Songe d'hiver" there is an extraordinary panorama of titles: *Vénus Aphrodite, Anadyomène, Vénus Urania, Vénus Acidalie, Cypris, Vénus Praxis, Vénus Coliade, Vénus Barbata, Vénus Argynnis, Vénus Victrix sans bras, Vénus Mélanide,* and *Vénus Callipyge,* to name only some in this tribute to the Venus of mythology and art.

For Darío, Venus is the Olympian figuration of the desire for eternal feminine beauty; although mortal women lose their beauty with age, she does not suffer these earthly changes. Darío clearly explains in the "Coloquio de los centauros" why Venus will always reign:

. . . . ¡Venus impera!
Ella es entre las reinas celestes la primera,
pues es quien tiene el fuerte poder de la Hermosura.

In "Mi tía Rosa" (1913) the parents of the young lover cannot understand his juvenile love and the poems to his sweetheart. On the other hand, his Aunt Rose advises him not to lose the most beautiful years of his life; in an exaltation of love and beauty we see the aunt transformed into Venus in one of Darío's most original passages:

— ¡Yo soy la inmortal Anadiómena, la gloriosa patrona de los cisnes! Yo soy la maravilla de las cosas, cuya presencia conmueve los nervios arcanos del orbe; yo soy la divina Venus, emperatriz de los reyes, madre de los poetas; mis pupilas fueron más poderosas que el entrecejo de Júpiter, y he encadenado a Pan con mi cinturón. La Primavera es mi clarín heráldico, y la Aurora mi timbalera. Murieron los dioses del Olimpo de Grecia, menos la única inmortal; y todas las otras divinidades podrán desaparecer mientras mi rostro alegrará por siempre la esfera. (*CC*, 334-335)

Darío proclaims the superiority of Venus, sovereign of sovereigns and inspiration of poets. Pan and all the other Olympian deities have given way to her. Only she remains eternal and her attractiveness will never diminish. Venus is the immortal invitation to the search for feminine charm.

In Banville's "La Rose" Venus also is depicted as the

sum total of beauty. She is asleep, a pose that is frequently treated in art. Eros spies her and contemplates her longingly:

> Et c'est la Rose! c'est la fleur tendre et farouche
> Qui présente à Cypris l'image de sa bouche,
> Et semble avoir un sang de pourpre sous sa chair.
> Fleur-femme, elle contient tout ce qui nous est cher,
> Jour, triomphe, caresse, embrassement, sourire:
> Voir la Rose, c'est comme écouter une lyre!

In spite of the detailed attention Banville pays Venus, he does not intimately identify his own sentiments with her symbolic meanings. To Banville, Venus is a symbol of great beauty that is strongly inspired in the plastic arts. In "Le démêloir," for example, he describes a woman as "pareille aux Vénus du grand peintre d'Anvers." Among Banville's many plastic descriptions of Venus, one is particularly effective. In "L'exil des dieux" we read:

> Mais, dénoués, épars, ses cheveux de soleil
> Tombent sur son épaule, et leur masse profonde
> Comme d'un fleuve d'or en fusion l'inonde.

She is the "adorable" queen of the Olympus "Avec son sein de rose et ses blancheurs d'étoile."

Venus has an equally plastic charm in Laprade's *Psyché;* she is frequently described as "la blanche Aphrodite," sometimes with "longues tresses d'or." Gautier, the original advocate of "la transposition d'art," decidedly writes guided by the plastic arts; in "Le poëme de la femme" he says:

> Pour Apelle ou pour Cléomène,
> Elle semblait, marbre de chair,
> En Vénus Anadyomène
> Poser nue au bord de la mer.

Venus enters into many of Darío's stories and poems. The following textual study will show that Venus as the symbol of beauty and amorous desire predominates. In "La ninfa" "surgió la ninfa del estanque, semejante a Citerea en su onda . . . ." In "El humo de la pipa" the protagonist sits smoking. With the first mouthful of smoke he dreams that he sees the ideal woman "con labios venusinos."[23] Here Venus is the symbol of carnal pleasure, of loving and being loved. Her name produces a mixture of emotions in the poet: that of the pure and ideal as well as the sensual. This reaction is again evident in "Luz de luna" (1893-97), where the figure of Pierrot-Darío, "el silencioso enamorado de luna," contemplates Selene-Moon: "Su cara expresaba la angustia; sus gestos, la desolación. Con su conocida mímica explicaba de qué modo se había quedado atrás; cómo sus compañeros le habían abandonado mientras él contemplaba, en un celestial éxtasis, el rostro de la luna . . . ." Darío's abysmal despair, which stems from the desires that Venus symbolizes and that the sight of Selene evokes, is completely opposed to the celestial ecstasy of Pierrot.[24] There is an interchange of the ideal and the sensual, a wandering from the Christian to the pagan that is present in his later works, but with reverse emphasis. Venus, symbol of love, is ubiquitous; merely contemplating the moon brings her to mind.

Compare "Venus" in *Azul* . . .; the lover again expresses his dual emotions:

¡Oh reina rubia! —dije—, mi alma quiere dejar su crisálida
y volar hacia ti, y tus labios de fuego besar;
y flotar en el nimbo que derrama en tu frente luz pálida,
y en siderales éxtasis no dejarte un momento de amar.

The sensual element is seen in "tus labios de fuego besar" and the ideal in "siderales éxtasis." But Venus says nothing, "Venus, desde el abismo, me miraba con triste mirar." The abyss is that of the lover who in vain tries to determine whether love is a "gracia celestial" or "pérfido obsequio de los abismos y su dueño."[25]

---

[23] Plowert, in his *Glossaire,* p. 96 gives the similar word *vénusté* 'qui est charmant comme Vénus,' found in Verlaine. Menéndez y Pelayo uses *venusinos* in the "Epístola a Horacio."

[24] The Pierrot theme is frequent in modern literature. See the *Cuentos,* p. 184, note 1.

[25] For an amplification of this point, see Salinas, *op. cit.,* pp. 56-57.

It is this same "pérfida mujer" that shows indifference to the poet in the portrait "El ideal" (1888):

> Sintió que la besaba con mis miradas
> y me castigó con la majestad de su belleza,
> y me vió como una reina y como una paloma.
> Pero pasó arrebatadora, triunfante, como
> una visión que deslumbra. Y yo, el pobre
> pintor de la Naturaleza y de Psiquis,
> hacedor de ritmos y de castillos aéreos,
> vi el vestido luminoso de la hada, la
> estrella de su diadema, y pensé en la
> promesa ansiada del amor hermoso. Mas
> de aquel rayo supremo y fatal, solo
> quedó en el fondo de mi cerebro un
> rostro de mujer, un sueño azul.

As a cloud passes in front of the moon, the poet catches a fleeting glimpse of Selene-Moon, "el vestido luminoso" and "la estrella de su diadema" that leads him to ponder once more Eros's promises of that longed for "amor hermoso." The tone, however, is a little less bitter than in "Luz de luna."

In the poem in prose "A una estrella" the poet is again in a state of ecstasy. The tone is one of awe or reverent fear set by the recurring phrase "¡quién besara tus labios luminosos!" or "Cuántas veces mi espíritu quiso volar hacia ti y quedó desalentado." Once, on contemplating her, he thought of divine love:

> Me hablaste del camino de la Gloria, donde hay que andar descalzo sobre cambroneras y abrojos; y desnudo, bajo una eterna granizada; y a oscuras, cerca de hondos abismos, llenos de sombra como la muerte. Me hablaste del vergel Amor, donde es casi imposible cortar una rosa sin morir, porque es rara la flor en que no anida un áspid. Y me dijiste de la terrible y muda esfinge de bronce que está a la entrada de la tumba . . . Y ya presa de mi desesperanza, de mi triste lugar de labor . . .

The surprising thing is that Venus-star shows compassion rather than indifference: "Entonces fué, adorable y blanca princesa, cuando tuviste compasión de aquel pobre poeta, y le miraba con tu mirada inefable y le sonreíste, y de tu sonrisa emergía el divino verso de la esperanza! Estrella mía, que estás tan lejos, ¡quién besara tus labios luminosos!" The lover stands fascinated by the serene beauty of Venus: "A través de un ramaje te contemplé en tu deleitable serenidad, y vi sobre los árboles negros trémulos hilos de luz como si hubiesen caído de la altura hebras de tu cabellera. Princesa del divino imperio azul, ¡quién besara tus labios luminosos!" It is almost the platonic beauty of God, the beauty of the world penetrated by the Divine idea. Venus, pure beauty, plays the principal role here, not Venus, carnal pleasure. However, one must mention the phrase "¡quién besara tus labios luminosos!" This is not at all platonic. She continues to be Venus, however pure and distant she may be.

Darío employs the various myths that have grown about Venus to give a delicate touch. In "Bouquet" the poet emphasizes the beauty of the rose: "A Venus, la llaman los poetas rósea," an allusion that we saw might well be Virgilian. There are other references to Venus in this same light tone. In "Las razones de Ashavero" (1893) the poet, disturbed by the threat of imperialism, goes about inquiring which is the best form of government. The star Venus is in agreement with the rose: "No tengo más opinión que ésta: la Belleza está sobre todo." In "Respecto a Horacio," a glorification of the poet, Lydia declares that Venus is the sovereign of the kingdom of love: ". . . me gozo en deshojar esta flor en nombre de Venus, mi reina."

Darío's most plastic portrayal of Venus has to do with her birth. This marvelous event, first related by Hesiod, has been taken up in art and is most celebrated in Botticelli's *Birth of Venus* and in works by Boucher and Albani. Venus's birth has also been hailed in modern poetry, in Laurent Tailhade's "Hymne à Aphrodite," Leconte de Lisle's "Khirôn," Heredia's "La naissance d'Aphrodite" and in Sully Prudhomme's "Naissance de Vénus." The latter is written in the first person. Venus speaks with great self-assurance of her mission in the world:

> Je parais, pour changer, reine des harmonies,
> Les rages du chaos en flottantes langueurs ;
> Car je suis la Beauté: des chaînes infinies
> Glissent de mes doigts blancs au plus profond des coeurs.

She concludes with a pithy summation of her worth, "J'apporte le bonheur à tout être qui sent."

Heredia offers a matter-of-fact account of Venus's arrival:

> L'Océan s'entr' ouvrit, et dans sa nudité
> Radieuse, émergeant de l'écume embrasée,
> Dans le sang d'Ouranos fleurit Aphrodité.

Mendès is even more succinct in his comments on Venus's birth; in *Bacchus* he says:

> Chère Cypris, Cypris compatissante,
> O vierge d'or, que chantèrent, premiers,
> Quand tu naquis de la mer blanchissante,
>   Les tendres ramiers !

It is in Leconte de Lisle's version that we observe more of a pictorial quality, with many of the details that can be seen in the most famous paintings on the subject:

> Sur la neige des mers Aphrodite, en riant,
> Comme un rêve enchanté, voguait vers l'Orient . . .
> De sa conque, flottant sur l'onde qui l'arrose,
> La nacre aux doux rayons reflétait son corps rose,
> Et l'Euros caressait ses cheveux déroulés,
> Et l'écume baisait ses pieds immaculés,
> Les Kharites en rond sur la mer murmurante
> Emperlaient en nageant leur blancheur transparente,
> Et les Rires légers, dans leurs jeunes essors,
> Guidaient la Conque bleue et ses divins trésors !

Darío's version of Venus's birth in the "Coloquio de los centauros" is closer to Leconte de Lisle's than to any of his other models. But, the commentary in Ménard and his reproductions of Albani's and Boucher's works must be acknowledged as a parallel source. Regardless of Darío's inspiration, these verses exceed in delicacy and plasticity any of his possible models. In lines that are some of Darío's most beautiful we see that Venus was born to triumph even over Jupiter:

Cuando del sacro abuelo la sangre luminosa
con la marina espuma formara nieve y rosa,
hecha de nieve y rosa nació la Anadiomena.
Al cielo alzó los brazos la lírica sirena;
los curvos hipocampos sobre las verdes ondas
lavaron los hocicos, y caderas redondas,
tritónicas melenas y dorsos de delfines
junto a la reina nueva se vieron. Los confines
del mar llenó el grandioso clamor; el Universo
sintió que un nombre armónico, sonoro como un verso,
llenaba el hondo hueco de la altura: ese nombre
hizo gemir la tierra de amor: fué para el hombre
más alto que el de Jove, y los númenes mismos
lo oyeron asombrados; los lóbregos abismos
tuvieron una gracia de luz. ¡Venus impera!

We know that it is actually over Darío that Venus reigns. It is not by chance that she, of all the Olympian deities, predominates, for Darío makes a cult of woman. Venus, the eternal symbol of woman, is essential to perfume life:

. . . la vida es bella
por poseer
la perla, la rosa, la estrella
y la mujer.

In this longing for possession, Darío's concept of woman as a vital force is again apparent. The mystery of the universe is concentrated in her. Hence, the endless search for Venus, further echoed in "¡Carne, celeste carne de la mujer!"

Eva y Cipris concentran el misterio
del corazón del mundo.

Venus and Eve, the height of womanliness in the pagan and Christian worlds, epitomize the whole mystery of life. Important recent documents on Darío contain verses that solidify the singular importance of Venus to Darío:

Mas sabed que de amor fragante
Venus es luz:

mas es un divino diamante
Cristo en la cruz.

Yo no sé en que dulce horizonte
nunca he podido separar
a Cristo en su cruz en el monte
y a mi Venus sobre la mar.[26]

Diana. In the works of Darío studied the goddess of the
moon and of hunting appears most often with her Roman
name; there is no mention of the Greek Artemis. *Selene* and
Hécate are used occasionally. These last two designations require a brief explanation. Neither originally belonged to Diana
or Artemis, the twin sister of Apollo. Selene was a moon
goddess, to be sure, but not connected with Apollo-Sun. She
was the sister of Helios, the sun god with whom Apollo became confused. As for Hecate, with whom the later poets
identified Artemis, she was the goddess of the dark of the
moon. With her baying hounds, Hecate was a dreaded creature.

Diana, then, played many roles. She was the beautiful
huntress, the chaste maiden and the lovely moon as well as
the divinity who became associated with the lower world and
the evil of dark nights. Diana, perhaps more than any other
divinity, represents the mixture of good and evil seen in all
the gods.

All of Diana's names are found in Darío's models. In
"L'exil des dieux" Banville calls her *Artémis;* in "Une femme
de Rubens," *Diane.* In Laprade's *Psyché* the Roman Diana
appears in her most well-known capacity, "armé d'arcs et de
flèches;" in "Éleusis" it is the Greek Artemis that Laprade
identifies with the hunt: "Les meutes d'Artémis." Leconte de
Lisle again stands out for the variety of names he has at his
command. In *Poèmes antiques Diane* is also *Kyllène, Séléné,
Phoebé* and *Artémis.* In Quintana's "La danza" we have the
familiar image of Diana followed by her nymphs. In Valera's

[26] See Evelyn C. Uhrhan, "Notes on the Seminario-Archivo de Rubén
Darío," *Kentucky Foreign Language Quarterly,* VIII (1961), 37-41.

poem "El dios Apolo" the goddess of the hunt is *Artemis;* in "Fábula de Euforión" she is *Selene* and *Diana.*

Darío's presentation of Diana is striking in that she, more so than any other divinity, appears as an object of art, with emphasis on her whiteness and chastity. Her beauty inspires a joy in contemplation with almost no suggestion of a longing for possession. The one possible exception to this attitude is in "Retrato de Watteau" (1887), where Diana as a type of adornment popular in eighteenth-century France, "se alza irresistible y desnuda sobre su plinto." "Virgen" and "blanca" abound in Darío's descriptions of her, which follow the traditional notion of Diana as the ideal of austere maiden beauty. She is the lovely mythological huntress, usually accompanied by her hounds. In this manner Rubens, Goujon and Saint-Gaudens have portrayed her in painting and in sculpture. Darío's concept of Diana's beauty seems more akin to that of Goujon and Saint-Gaudens than to the rather Amazon-like proportions of Rubens.

Diana is the divine huntress in several of Darío's stories and poems. In "Carta del país azul" the poet, on leaving the church where he has just prayed, bursts into a lyric exaltation of life and the senses as he contemplates the sculptor's statues: "El asceta había desaparecido de mí: quedaba el pagano . . . Amo la belleza, gusto del desnudo; de las ninfas de los bosques, blancas y gallardas; de Venus en su concha y de Diana, la virgen cazadora de carne divina, que va entre su tropa de galgos, con el arco en comba, a la pista de un ciervo o de un jabalí." Here, as in "El velo de la reina Mab" (1887) with the opposition between "el torso de Diana y el rostro de la Madona" we see the duality that foreshadows the future conflict. In "Arte y hielo" (1888) the virgen huntress is one of the proud sculptor's boasts: "Ahí está la virgen diosa cazadora como si estuviese viva, inmaculada y blanca."

Diana is depicted in a similar manner in the poetry of *Azul* . . .; in "Primaveral" she is part of the scene on an amphora:

En el ánfora está Diana,
real, orgullosa y esbelta,
con su desnudez divina
y en actitud cinegética.

The characterization in the last two verses is almost identical
to the portrayal of Diana in the poem to J. J. Palma, also in
Azul . . .:

Pinta las dulces Gracias, o la desnuda Europa,
en el pulido borde de un vaso de marfil,
o a Diana, diosa virgen de desceñida ropa,
con aire cinegético, o en grupo pastoril.

The abduction of one of Diana's nymphs from her bath
is an event that has fascinated poet and painter alike. Such
notable artists as Titian, Albani, Domenichino and Solimena
interpreted this theme. In the Ovidian "Palimpsesto" of
Prosas profanas Diana in her bath is "blanca y desnuda como
una estrella." However, here Darío is emphasizing not her
whiteness, but her unwavering virtue. When a centaur steals
one of Diana's nymphs, she loses her serene repose; "terrible,
fiera," much like the Artemis Banville describes in "L'exil des
dieux," she pursues the bold abductor. Darío wishes to leave
no doubt that she is the rigid defender of feminine virtue, for
he inserts an original note not found in the *Metamorphoses*.
"La casta diosa de la venganza" was not satisfied to kill only
the kidnapper:

Llegan las ninfas. Lloran. ¿Qué ven?
En la carrera la cazadora
con su saeta castigadora
a la robada mató también.

The purification of the nymph through death has unquestion-
ably established Diana as the model of chastity.

This vision of her uncompromising virtue intensifies the
philistine incomprehension of art in "Arte y hielo"; the people
are stunned by the nude statue of Diana that goes out into the
streets to seek bread for the hungry sculptor: "Diana salió, y
con ser casta diva, produjo un ¡oh! de espanto en la ciudad . . .
Y esa curva saliente de un brazo, y esa redondez del hombro y

147

ese vientre ¿no son una profanación?" It is in "La Miss" (1893) that Darío establishes what is profane: "El desnudo condenado por la castidad no es el de la virginal Diana, . . . es el desnudo de Salomé la danzarina, o el de la señorita Nini *Patte en l'air,* profesora de coreografía y de otras cosas." This same idea, certainly not new, is expressed in a similar mythological framework in Laprade's "Éleusis":

> Vous fuirez les regards des ouvriers profanes,
> O Nymphes qui veniez en des nuits diaphanes,
> Vous tenant par la main, formant des pas en rond,
> Les cheveux dénoués et des fleurs sur le front,
> Sans que rien lui voilât vos beautés ingénues,
> Devant l'artiste saint poser chastes et nues.

That Diana was unyielding and beyond all temptation is manifest. There is but one episode, which belongs more properly to Selene the moon goddess, in which Diana was attracted to a young man. She spied handsome Endymion sleeping on Mt. Latmos where he fed his flock. Selene, enraptured, came down, kissed him and spent the rest of the night watching over him, a ritual that was repeated regularly thereafter. In the "Dedicatoria" of the *Poema del otoño* (1907) Darío recounts this myth:

> y apenas envuelta en los velos
> de la ilusión,
> baja a los bosques de los cielos
> por Endimión.

The one incident in which Diana showed any warmth of emotion also interests Laprade in "Éleusis." He, too, insists upon her as completely virtuous:

> . . . . . . Sa beauté solitaire,
> Vierge pour tous les dieux, garde ses doux secrets
> Au seul Endymion, fils rêveur des forêts.

The assimilation of Hecate's personality to Diana's is not apparent in Darío. Hecate remains the morbid goddess of the night, who, accompanied by her dogs, haunts graves. Undoubtedly, Diana and Hecate are maintained distinct from each other in Darío's mind by reason of the great beauty Diana represents for him. In the "Dedicatoria":

> Hécate hace aullar los mastines;
> mas Diana es bella,

IV   Divinities Presiding Over the Arts

Apolo. The god of music and poetry appears in Darío's works with many names: *Apolo, Foibos, Febo, Helios, Hiperión, Sol* and *Musagetes*.[27] Again this wealth of names is matched only by Leconte de Lisle, in whose *Poèmes antiques* we find *Apollon, Phoïbos, Phoebos, Phoebos-Apollon, Hèlios* and *Hypérion*. When Darío is speaking of the god of music or poetry, it is solely *Apolo,* not *Foibos* or any equivalent that he uses. The other designations for Apollo retain their original idea of him as the god of light; however, once, in the "Coloquio de los centauros," *Apolo* refers to the god of light.

Apollo's role runs a broad gamut, from a statue in "Carta del país azul" (1888) to what seems to be *Apolo-Helios-Cristo* in a later poem "Helios" (1905). Venus and Apollo, the ideals of feminine and masculine beauty respectively, are accordingly symbols of the height of the sculptor's accomplishments in "Carta del país azul": "De una cantera evoca y crea cien dioses. Y con su cincel destroza las angulosidades de la piedra bronca y forma el seno de Afrodita o el torso del padre Apolo." Similarly, Mendès offers Apollo as the epitome of masculine beauty in his chapter called "Nécessité d'être beau" in *L'art d'aimer*. For Darío, though, Apollo is largely the poet and musician par excellence as in "El sátiro sordo"; no greater tribute can be paid to Orpheus and his music than to have Venus mistake him for Apollo. As a culmination of the eulogy to Orpheus and, at the same time, a derision of the satyr's insensitivity, "Venus, que pasaba por las cercanías, preguntó de lejos con su divina voz: '¿Está aquí acaso Apolo?' " Apollo's

[27] In Spanish Apollo as the leader of the Muses is called *Musageta* <L. *Musagetes,* Donadíu y Puignan, *op. cit.,* III, 706. Darío uses the Latin form in the "Canto a la Argentina."

pre-eminence in musical skills is delightfully and originally expressed in "Las siete bastardas de Apolo" (1903). The notes of the musical scale reveal, "Somos siete hijas bastardas del rey Apolo."

However, Darío's disgust for materialism and the "reyes burgueses" provokes a momentary disenchantment even with Apollo that is whimsically and fantastically set forth in "En la batalla de las flores" (1893). The plight of the poet is indeed tragic; not even Apollo can earn a living by playing his lyre and writing poetry. In this story Apollo is the typical business man; he now carries a briefcase instead of a lyre:

> La verdad es que si dejamos el Olimpo, no hemos abandonado la Tierra. ¡Tiene tantos encantos para los mismos dioses! Unos hemos tenido buena suerte; otros muy mala: no he sido yo de los más afortunados. Con la lira debajo del brazo he recorrido casi todo el mundo. Cuando no pude vivir en Atenas me fuí a París; allí he luchado mucho tiempo, sin poder hacer gran cosa. ¡Con deciros que he sido, en la misma capital del arte, fámulo y mandadero de un bibliopola decadente! Me decidí a venir a América, a probar fortuna, y un buen día desembarqué en la Ensenada, en calidad de inmigrante. Me resolví a no hacer un solo verso, y en efecto: soy ya rico y estanciero.

Apollo complains that those who call themselves poets are too concerned with the practical life. He is shocked at those who leave a sonnet without the last tercet "por ir a averiguar en la Bolsa un asunto de tanto por ciento." The irony of the situation is that Apollo himself is guilty of this very thing, for on being asked whether he no longer wished to write poetry, he replied with a secretive air, as if he did not wish the truth to become common knowledge:

> — Aquí *inter nos* —respondióme—, he de confesar que no he dejado de ocuparme en mi viejo oficio. En ciertas horas, cuando el bullicio de los negocios se calma y mis cuentas quedan en orden, dejo este disfraz de hombre moderno, y voy a hacer algunas estrofas en compañía de los silfos de la noche y de los cisnes de los estanques.

The affected and consequently humorous use of Latin adds to the picture of Apollo as just another pompous "rey burgués."

But even in Darío's latest works, Apollo symbolizes the immortality of art and Darío's devotion to it. In the "Pequeño poema de Carnaval" (1907) Darío answers Lugones' query concerning Darío's slackened literary output:

> ¡Pues Apolo es eterno
> y el arte es inmortal!
> . . . .
> Sepa la Primavera
> que mi alma es compañera
> del sol que ella venera
> y del supremo Pan,
> Y que si Apolo ardiente
> la llama, de repente,
> contestará: ¡Presente,
> mi capitán!

Prior to 1897 there are only a few references to Apollo as the god of light. The time of day is poetically expressed in "Coloquio de los centauros" (1896): "Mas he aquí que Apolo se acerca al meridiano." Similarly, in "El faisán" (1896) we find:

> por una ventana vi que un negro manto
> de nube, de Febo cubría el encanto.

It is in the compositions after 1897 that allusions to Apollo as *Foibos* and *Helios* are found. (The *oi* of Darío's *Foibos* is perhaps an imitation of Leconte de Lisle's *Phoïbos*.) There is a significance to the evocation of Apollo as the god of light in Darío's later works. He may be the pagan god of light, but he really embodies the Christian idea of the Light of the world. In the opening lines of "Helios" (1905) it is merely *Helios* or *Hiperionida* who "lleva la rienda asida." Then we have the figure of Helios-Apollo in the role of Saviour:

> ¡Helios! Portaestandarte
> de Dios, padre del Arte,
> la paz es imposible, mas el amor eterno.
> Danos siempre el anhelo de la vida,
> y una chispa sagrada de tu antorcha encendida
> con que esquivar podamos la entrada del infierno.

151

The spiritual meaning Darío attaches to Helios is a departure from strict fact. Apollo, we are told, should not be confused with Helios, a god of the older dynasty, who represented the sun in its physical rather than spiritual manifestations.[28] There is a similar image in *Canto a la Argentina* (1910). Darío, in a long plea to the sun, requests its blessings for Argentina. However, in the first of the verses below Darío seems more certainly to be invoking an indigenous god:

> ¡Oh Sol! ¡Oh padre teogónico!
> ¡Sol símbolo que irradias
> en el pabellón! Salomónico
> y helénico, lumbre de Arcadias,
> mítico, incásico, mágico!
> ¡Foibos, triunfantet en el trágico
> vencimiento de las sombras;
>
> . . . .
>
> que perdure tu portento
> que el orbe todo ilumina
>
> . . . .
>
> ¡Foibos, triunfante en el trágico
> del creciente pensamiento.

Another of the divinities has undergone a transformation.

Musa (Corominas: *musa* is first documented in Alonso Fernández de Palencia (1490). This word is highly common in Darío's models, both French and Spanish. It is found in Meléndez Valdés' *Odas* and, of course, in "Elegía a la musas," one of Moratín's best poems. Quintana, Bello, Valera and Menéndez y Pelayo use this word frequently as do Laprade, Leconte de Lisle, Banville and Heredia.)

The number of the muses, not specified in Homer, is usually taken to be nine as in Hesiod's *Theogony*. At first, they were not distinguished from each other. Hesiod describes them as being of one mind, their hearts set upon song. This is the frame of reference in "Las siete bastardas de Apolo"; the musical notes' voices are so beautiful that except for their lesser number, they would have been taken for the Muses: "Al

---

[28] See Gayley, *The Classic Myths,* p. 27.

hablar, su lenguaje era musical; y si hubiesen sido nueve, habría creído seguramente que eran las musas del sagrado Olimpo." In another story, "Bouquet," they are portrayed in a delicately plastic image in their role as companions to Venus: "Venus y las Musas la buscan [la rosa] por valiosa y por garrida."

Most important of all to Darío are the Muses as poetic inspiration, but preferably "las musas de carne y hueso" as seen in *El canto errante.* In the "Balada" Darío first enumerates the charm of each muse; in later times each one presided over her own branch of the arts and sciences. Darío defines their respective spheres in verses that marvelously rise above a trite enumeration:

> Clío está en esta frente hecha de Aurora,
> Euterpe canta en esta lengua fina,
> Talía ríe en la boca divina,
> Melpómene es ese gesto que implora;
> en estos pies Terpsícore se adora,
> cuello inclinado es de Erato embeleso,
> Polimnia intenta a Caliope proceso
> por esos ojos en que Amor se quema.
> Urania rige todo ese sistema.

Notwithstanding these many charms, the virtues of the "musa de carne y hueso" are extolled:

> Líricos cantan y meditan sabios:
> por esos pechos y por esos labios.
> ¡La mejor musa es la de carne y hueso!

It is the same idea of the possessive value of woman that is so powerfully expressed in "¡Carne, celeste carne de la mujer!" and in Darío's utilization of the swan motif. This concept, vitally entrenched in his evaluation of woman, is indispensable to an understanding of his marked preference for certain mythological figures.

The underlying purpose in our study of the divinities was to reveal the transformation that Darío's mythology underwent around 1897. In such stories as "La leyenda de San Martín" (1897), "La fiesta de Roma" (1898) and "Palimpsesto II" (1908) we have seen an ascent of Christianity over paganism.

In his prose prior to 1897, in "Rojo" (1892) and "El velo de la reina Mab" (1887), we saw signs that prefigured this change. The same phenomenon in his mythology is observed in *Prosas profanas* and *Cantos de vida y esperanza* as well as in his later poetry. In "Responso a Verlaine" of *Prosas profanas* there is a triumph of Christianity over the sensual and pagan in the last lines:

> Y el Sátiro contemple sobre un lejano monte,
> Una cruz que se eleva cubriendo el horizonte
> ¡Y un resplandor sobre la cruz!

There has been a leveling of Christian and pagan figures whereby the Olympian personages serve to express the Christianity of the "pagan" poet.[29] Rome comes to signify the two worlds as we saw in "Palimpsesto II" with the development of the pagan flute into the cathedral organ. With the advance of time, Christ became more present in Darío's spirit.

But, even in his later years there are momentary regressions in which the pagan charms reassert themselves. In "Canción de otoño en primavera" (1905), although there is the mature realization that "abrazo y beso" are no longer the synthesis of eternity, Darío confesses "mi sed de amor no tiene fin." Here we have one of the two reasons for his lasting, though lessened, fascination with the pagan world. We know that his search for love, beauty and woman is fulfilled in Venus. We are told in "Mi tía Rosa" that she, of all the divinities, is the one enduring figure. The reason for her eternal reign is stated in the "Coloquio de los centauros": she has the power of beauty, a beauty that will never die.

The second reason also involves beauty, but as seen in the

[29] Dr. Antonio Belmas, in *Este otro Rubén Darío*, Barcelona, 1960, p. 165 quotes a statement of Unamuno's that shows great understanding on the part of Unamuno towards the allegedly "pagan" poet: "Se conocía, y ante Dios —¡y hay que saber lo que era Dios para aquella suprema flor espiritual de la indianidad!— hundía su corazón en el polvo de la tierra, en el polvo pisado por los pecadores. Se decía algunas veces pagano, pero yo os digo que no lo era.

No descansó nunca aquel su pobre corazón sediento de amor. No de amar, sino de que se le amase."

"Pequeño poema de carnaval" (1907). Apollo is eternal because he is the mythological incarnation of art. Moreover, Darío's soul will always be a companion to Pan, for "luz" and "furia" are a gift of Pan. Certain divinities offer artistic inspiration and suggestions of great physical beauty; as such, they are fascinating. In the light of these facts, we can better understand the vacillations in Darío's later works and his brief returns to the land of nymphs as in "Las tres reinas magas" (1912). Here he chooses the land of myrrh, but then, "tras las arboledas vense cruzar formas blancas perseguidas por seres velludos de pies hendidos." In general, though, the tone of the second period in his mythology is radically different from the atmosphere of the era of *Azul* . . . in that the "fiestas galantes" are subordinated to an agonized pondering of his personal destiny, best exemplified perhaps by "Spes," "Dulzura del ángelus" or "Soneto pascual" (1915) where Christ is a desirable but elusive goal:

> de la Virgen, el Niño y el San José proscripto;
> y yo, en mi pobre burro, caminando hacia Egipto,
> y sin la estrella ahora, muy lejos de Belén.

His last important poem, "Pax" (1915), evidences his ultimate faith in Christ. Although, like any orthodox Christian, he cannot be certain of his personal destiny, he admits to the Divine Providence of God:

> y contra el homicidio, el odio, el robo
> Él es la Luz, el Camino y la Vida.

Darío's life seems to have ended on a decidedly Christian, if not Catholic, note.

CHAPTER VI

CONCLUSION

Darío was a cultured, well-read person, but decidedly not a scholar. His view of Greece and Rome was more owing to his French and, to a lesser degree, to his Spanish readings than to a firsthand knowledge of classical texts. These he knew, to some extent, in translation. The analysis of his Latin quotations has interestingly revealed a preponderance of Biblical, not classical references. The latter, we observed, are those that would be known to a person with a basic Latin training. Yet, to label them the most memorable bits of Horace, Virgil and Ovid would be misleading, for they were most likely not Darío's fond recollection of his youthful readings, but rather the result of his having returned in later years, under the stimulus of his French readings, to those classical texts he had known earlier.

The predominant Biblical quotations are, for the most part, expressive of Darío's overwhelming fear of death and his concern for salvation. His strict religious upbringing has to be a factor in explaining these particular quotations; the Biblical ones with a sensual connotation, however, seem to be the exclusive influence of a similar tendency in French literature during the last half of the nineteenth century. Throughout these Latin quotations, Darío seems to show a bit of stylistic pleasure in displaying his "erudition" that at times exceeds his accuracy in spelling, syntax and word order. Apart from the Biblical-sensual Latin quotations, Darío had many models in both Spanish and French literature for the insertion of Latin words and, for that matter, words from other foreign languages.

In general, the importance of Darío's French models has been somewhat overstated. Much of the "newness" in his writings has been too blithely explained in terms of the Parnassians

157

and, in particular, Leconte de Lisle. It has, for example, been said that Darío was introduced to the world of Greco-Roman mythology by his modern French readings. Some of his familiarity with that tradition is certainly a result of those readings. However, documentation throughout has demonstrated that Darío had earlier been exposed to it during his adolescent readings of Spanish literature, especially those of the Golden Age and the eighteenth and nineteenth centuries. Although French poetry undoubtedly was the impetus for incorporating these elements into his works, Spanish was very present in his background. Garcilaso, Góngora, Quintana, Valera and Menéndez y Pelayo are among those Spanish authors who cannot be discounted. The evidence presented indicates beyond all reasonable doubt that Darío's Greco-Roman vocabulary has to be viewed as the merging of two traditions, the "castizo" and the Parnassian.

The comparison of Darío's mythological portrayals with those of his French models has, in a sense, minimized his indebtedness even further, for he brilliantly sets himself apart from all others by his individual style in delineating the Greco-Roman divinities. We saw that the plasticity of Darío's images is at times so intense that he seems more surely to have been inspired by a representation in art than by any literary model. For some time, the museums were as important to poets as the libraries. Banville, in his *Petit traité de versification française* (1872), had called poetry the only complete art, for it contained all the others; Gautier, in his *Histoire du romantisme* (1874), rejoiced at the introduction of the plastic arts into poetry. Above all, though, the most significant distinguishing characteristic of Darío's images based on mythology is that these figures are animated with his own sentiments. His "culto por la belleza" inspired his love of the Greco-Roman world; the elements of beauty in that culture acquire new force in Darío's writings. The nymphs attain extraordinarily pictorial force in "Acuarela" with "sus manos gráciles de ninfa." Moreover his amorous inclinations led him to that distant world, which offered an erotic climate that effectively stimulated his imagination. Salinas appropriately remarked that "lo griego" was for Darío not "un objeto de conocimiento" but rather "un norte para deseos sueltos en busca de rumbo."

Then too, the erotic can be purged of all vulgarity when expressed within a mythological frame of reference. When Darío uses mythological figures to speak of universal emotions, it is because these sentiments can, in this way, be expressed more purely and intensely. Lastly, the impersonality of these people is often advantageous; the personal aspect of Darío's preoccupations is elevated to a sphere of universality when transferred to beings both distant and noble. His many laments concerning the plight of the artist in the world rise above being a mere personal complaint or grudge. Moreover, the names of the divinities are not empty and devoid of meaning. On the contrary, they have an evocative power that excites the imagination and recalls an endless number of meanings.

We have seen throughout that the "grecolatinizante" atmosphere, beautifully adapted to the sometimes sculptured prose of the "cuentos," shows Darío's feeling for "lo precioso y exquisito" without being merely ornamental. After 1897, the stories reveal a change in the role of mythology; the Greco-Roman personalities now express Darío's belief in Christianity. His search for himself is reflected in his works. In "La leyenda de San Martín" (1897) the boy born in a pagan land has felt the flame of Christianity since childhood; the evolution of Lucio Varo in "La fiesta de Roma" (1898) is not unlike Darío's. The sad hour of Calvary in the story "Palimpsesto I" (1893) has been converted into glorious triumph.

The interplay of the Christian and pagan, we noted, is not an isolated phenomenon of the stories. It has also been observed in *Prosas profanas, Cantos de vida y esperanza* and his later poetry, with the vacillations also typical of the "cuentos." In "Divina Psiquis" (1905):

> Entre la catedral y las ruinas paganas
> Vuelas, ¡oh, Psiquis, oh, alma mía!

The beauty and sensuality of the pagan world and its artistic stimulus do not completely cease to charm Darío; however, in his last important poem, "Pax" (1915), he declares his faith in Christ.

It must be acknowledged, then, that the myths in Darío's hands were not distant and impersonal as they were for the Parnassians. The stylized, mural-like portrayals of Heredia's *Les trophées* and the marmoreal scenes of Leconte de Lisle's *Poèmes antiques* offered only a point of departure for Darío; his own moods, ranging from the frivolous to the reflective, are infused into the mythical beings. The myths become intimately identified with feeling and theme; in this respect, Darío diverges from his models, French and Spanish alike.

The problem of establishing sources is precarious, especially when dealing with a poet as complex as Darío, and, above all, if one aims at literal precision as Marasso sometimes did in his creditable study. We have pointed out on many occasions that at times Darío's sources are so interwoven and so well amalgamated that it is impossible to speak with certitude. Nonetheless, the chapters on the divinities demonstrated that the voluptuous air, the atmosphere of eighteenth-century France, is much more intense in Darío than in Verlaine's *Fêtes galantes*. Moreover, that tone in Darío, so often pointed to as an influence of Verlaine, could well have come from other French authors, most notably Banville, who earlier echoed those sentiments in their works. In fact, Banville's "Les jardins" (1867) predates by two years Verlaine's "Le faune," one of the poems from *Fêtes galantes* most quoted to illustrate Darío's source of inspiration. (See *silvano.*) Although Darío delighted in creating voluptuous scenes, he never descended to the vulgarities of some of his French models such as Laprade, Silvestre and Mallarmé.

Leconte de Lisle exercised great influence upon the other Parnassians. He was also important to Darío, especially with reference to the Greek transliterations and the words in *-ida*. However, apart from these, such "vocablos exóticos" as *ánfora, clámide* and *siringa* are not so clearly due to Leconte de Lisle. They are found earlier, for example, in Laprade, whose "Éleusis" (1844) also has a description of Jupiter's affair with Leda. Leconte de Lisle's "Hélène" (1852) does not, therefore, mark the rebirth of the theme of the swan in French poetry.[1] Moreover, the very image "khlamyde d'or" that Leconte de Lisle uses to describe Apollo-Sun in "Le réveil d'Hèlios" and "Dies irae" had earlier been used by Laprade in "Éleusis" to describe Apollo. In short, Leconte de Lisle has too often been singled out as "the" influence on certain aspects of Darío's vocabulary. Darío responded to a combination of influences, both French and Spanish.

Our study of Darío's Greco-Roman vocabulary better enables us to situate this aspect of his style in its time. There was a pre-modernist atmosphere of exoticism, Oriental, German, Greco-Roman and French classic that prepared the way for the triumph of *Azul* . . . . In 1880 two pre-modernists published certain works that interest us. Adolfo Mitre, showing the influence of Gautier's "Poëme de la femme," wrote in a manner that recalls the adolescent, romantic Darío. It is only in isolated elements and not at all in tone that the later Darío is anticipated:

> . . . No me escondas
> tu desnudez sublime y opulenta.
> Friné sale desnuda de las ondas,
> y el arte que maneja los pinceles
> para su gloria, desde entonces, cuenta
> la Venus Anadyómena de Apeles:
> ¡Quién sabe si no encuentro en tu hermosura
> un poema mejor que esa pintura![2]

In the same year Carlos Monsalve published his *Páginas literarias*. Here, though, the emphasis is on German fantasy. The Teutonic world was not new to Spanish literature. It had been seen earlier in Bécquer, an avid reader of Heine, in translation, and of Musset. Monsalve, more so than any of the other pre-modernists, showed a broad taste for the exotic. Thus

---

[1] Max Henríquez Ureña, *Breve historia*, p. 20, singles out the importance of "Hélène" in discussing this theme.

[2] Quoted by M. H. Lacau and M. Manacorda de Rosetti, "Antecedentes," p. 178.

in his poem "El dragón rojo" the setting is China; in "Ibrahim," Arabia and in "El precio del rescate," the Sahara desert. We mentioned earlier that the German motif also held a certain interest for Darío, but to a lesser degree by far than the Greco-Roman; it was in Jaimes Freyre's *Castalia bárbara* (1899) that German mythology was vigorously and enthusiastically evoked.

We now wish to turn to those poets closely associated with Darío to determine which ones were his precursors in using the Greco-Roman motif. The chronology will prove that it is not accurate to call them his precursors, for with the exception of one book by Leopoldo Díaz, it is Darío who preceded them in this taste. Since Díaz's *Sonetos* coincides in year with *Azul . . .*, we believe that Díaz's book is independent of any influence of Darío, unless Díaz had access to Darío's writings, particularly his stories, which were published in the newspapers. In *Sonetos* a marked tendency towards Greek themes is observed. There is an exaltation of Greece in terms of some of her personages: Aeschylus, Homer and Sophocles. In these poems there is quite a similarity to Leconte de Lisle's treatment of that civilization. Moreover, other sonnets by Díaz display pictorial qualities that introduce the "transposition d'art" that was later to be developed in Modernism. "El fauno" is one of this kind, here quoted in part to illustrate certain pre-Parnassian characteristics:

> Entre la sombra del follaje hundido
> esconde el viejo fauno su figura,
> y acecha cauteloso en la espesura
> la blanca ninfa que su pecho ha herido.
>
> Brillan sus ojos lúbricos. El nido
> le habla de amor, el viento le murmura
> cálidas frases, y en la selva oscura
> Amo en ti la hermosura esplenderosa,

In this poem there is a voluptuous air, a sensuality that brings this sonnet a bit closer to Darío's style than to the impersonal re-creations of Leconte de Lisle. On the whole, though, it seems that Díaz's poetry, similar to Mitre's, is romantic in atmosphere

162

regardless of lexical suggestions of Parnassianism. Some of their images are reminiscent of Laprade's mythological scenes. Consider, for example, "La estatua":

> Amo en ti la hermosura esplenderosa,
> la hermosura de Venus Afrodita,
> en donde un soplo cálido se agita
> como ardiente promesa voluptuosa.

It is not until 1892 that we see in Díaz the whole world of lesser divinities, fauns, satyrs, nymphs and naiads, that we see so abundantly in Darío beginning with *Azul* . . . . At this later date, Díaz was obviously writing under the influence of Darío.

To what extent, then, was Darío's partiality for the Greco-Roman world shared by Gutiérrez Nájera, Casal and Silva?[3] As we have seen to a limited extent in the case of Díaz, those early modernists were not precursors of Darío in this respect. In comparing the impact of Greco-Roman mythology on this group, Silva can almost be discounted. In his "Oración" we find "brazos de rosa," possibly an Anacreontic reminiscence. In "Realidad" there is brief and superficial reference to "la chipriota Venus." In "Luz de luna" and "Taller" there is an atmosphere mildly suggestive of eighteenth-century France. In Silva's story "La protesta de la musa" the poet's muse appears in a manner that recalls Gutiérrez Nájera's "Musa blanca." Silva's muse chastizes the desolate poet and his satires; Gutiérrez

3 Julio A. Leguizamón, *Historia de la literatura hispanoamericana,* Buenos Aires, 1945, II, 260, 277 and 285 presents Gutiérrez Nájera, Casal and Silva as pre-modernists. Prior to this group, he places Leopoldo Díaz as a prominent exponent of Parnassianism. Alfred Coester, *The Literary History of Spanish America,* New York, 1916, pp. 452, 455 sees Gutiérrez Nájera, Casal and Silva, for the most part, as precursors of Darío. Coester (p. 466) considers Díaz one of those who imitated Darío. Pedro Henríquez Ureña, *Las corrientes literarias,* pp. 171-172, divides Modernism into two periods. The first, from 1882-1896, includes Casal, Gutiérrez Nájera, Silva and Darío. Around Darío was formed the second group that is situated in the years from 1896-1920. Max Henríquez Ureña, *Breve historia,* sees none of these as precursors of Darío. Enrique Anderson Imbert, *Historia de la literatura hispanoamericana,* México, 1954, places Gutiérrez Nájera, Casal and Silva in the first generation of modernists along with Darío. However, on p. 264, Anderson Imbert states that Leopoldo Díaz was one of those in Argentina who created the movement that in 1893 was to hail Darío as the foremost poet of the language.

Nájera's comforts him in his sorrow over the loss of his sweetheart. The influence of Poe that Englekirk sees in Gutiérrez Nájera's poem seems also to be present in this work by Silva.[4]

Gutiérrez Nájera and Casal are the two in whom we find a lexicon that shows more of Darío's influence, though Gutiérrez Nájera is more akin to Darío than Casal is. In Gutiérrez Nájera's *Odas breves* (1893) we find a rather assorted group of Greco-Roman references: *bacante, ninfa, sirena, náyade, hamadriada, sátiro, néctar, ambrosía, cítara* and *canéfora*. His portrayal of these beings is plastic and objective:

> y, enfurecidos, a las blancas ninfas
> los sátiros caprípedos persiguen.

His plastic images of this type are like the Parnassians' in that they are faithful reproductions of the traditional aspects of the myths.

At any rate, Gutiérrez Nájera is more inclined to the Greco-Roman than Julián del Casal. Casal's preference is for the Oriental motif; consequently, his development of Greco-Roman myths is slight. In *Hojas al viento* (1890) we find only *bacante* in "Estatua de carne." In *Nieve* (1892) the *oceánidas,* in a poem of the same title, are addressed in a stylized manner as "ninfas del mar." In "Venus Anadyomena" the *delfín* and *nereida* figure in a description that is just barely suggestive of Botticelli's *Birth of Venus,* which later so marvelously inspired Darío. In Casal:

> Sentada, al pie de verdinegras moles,
> sobre la espalda de un delfín cetrino
> que de la aurora el rayo purpurino
> jaspea de brillantes tornasoles;
>
> envuelta en luminosos arreboles,
> Venus emerge el cuerpo alabastrino
> frente al húmedo borde del camino
> alfombrado de róseos caracoles.

[4] See John Eugene Englekirk, *Edgar Allan Poe in Hispanic Literature,* New York, 1934, pp. 245-246 concerning the Poesque influence on this poem by Gutiérrez Nájera.

Moviendo al aire las plateadas colas,
blancas nereidas surgen de las olas
y hasta la diosa de ojos maternales

llevan, entre las manos elevadas,
níveas conchas de perlas nacaradas,
ígneas ramas de fúlgidos corales.

In "Camafeo" there is the commonplace verse "y hay en tu voz acentos de sirena."

Báquicas canciones and *cisne* are the only Greco-Roman references in *Rimas* (1893). In this collection the whiteness of the swan is alluded to in "A la belleza" and "Neurosis." In the latter, it is Jupiter-Swan that appears: "del blanco cisne que amaba Leda." *Nieve* is the height of the Greco-Roman in Casal. In "Galatea" we find the gracelessly Anacreontic or possibly Virgilian allusion seen so frequently in Darío and once in Silva: "piel color de rosa." In addition to the references already quoted, there are certain pictorial poems that resemble the Parnassian treatment of mythology. "Prometeo" and "Las oceánidas" are both objective presentations with pictorial qualities of the myth of Prometheus. It is also in *Nieve* that we find "Venus Anadyomena" and "Júpiter y Europa," pictorial poetizations of myths, as well as "Hércules ante la hidra" and "Hércules y las estinfálides."

We may conclude, therefore, that the neo-Grecian air that was heralded by Darío in *Azul* . . . is imitated by this group in a more limited and less individual way. Almost absent in Casal's *Hojas al viento,* the Greco-Roman asserts itself more visibly in *Nieve*. This minimal amount of enthusiasm for that motif is even less apparent in *Rimas*. Here, the Greco-Roman has degenerated to uninspired evocations of the swan. Casal's modernist lexicon is more striking in *Nieve* and *Rimas* with respect to the many "esdrújulo" adjectives, some of which are *áureo* and *róseo,* and his repertoire of such substantives as *lirios, lotos, jaspe, ópalo* and *alabastro*. (With regard to the "esdrújulo" adjectives, Casal actually uses them as grave accented words, following the common tendency of everyday conversation to diphthongize the hiatus.)

In Casal, as well as in Gutiérrez Nájera, the use of Latin titles that was so popular in that period is seen. In *Hojas al viento* we find "Post umbra" and "In memoriam"; in *Nieve,* "Tristissima nox," "Pax animae" and the Baudelairian "Horridum somnium"; in *Rimas,* "Aegri somnia," "Laus noctis" and "O ¡altitudo!" [sic], a curious case of Spanish punctuation. In Silva we find only "Ars." Such exotic words as *ánfora* are absent in this group with the exception of *cítara* and *canéfora* in Gutiérrez Nájera. We also notice that the Greek transliterations and violent derivatives such as *kalofónico* that appear in Darío are not used by Silva, Casal or Gutiérrez Nájera.

Darío's originality cannot be denied, although for years it was dimmed by his imitators, the "rubendaríacos," who, with considerably less talent and taste, vulgarized this aspect of Darío. There was an epidemic of eighteenth-century frivolities, smiling princesses and graceless evocations of nymphs and fauns that caused a distorted estimate of Darío. Yet, the close study of that kind of imagery in Darío's works shows how, with limited recourse to the Greco-Roman and Spanish classics, and more under the influence of nineteenth-century French literature, Darío, even compared with the Spanish-American poets closest to him, stands out for the way he makes that Greco-Roman vocabulary distinctively his own. We have seen throughout that he employs it with flexibility and originality. He even ventures to create his own Greco-Roman words such as *pandórico, fáunico* and *kalofónico,* in seriousness and in jest, in prose and in verse, with the admirable agility with which he has always known how to harmonize models, sources and materials of the most varied origin.

A SELECTED BIBLIOGRAPHY

Alemán Bolaños, Gustavo, *Divulgaciones de Rubén Darío,* Nicaragua, 1958.

——, *La juventud de Rubén Darío (1890-1893),* Guatemala, 1923.

Alonso, Dámaso, *Estudios y ensayos gongorinos,* Madrid, 1955.

——, *La lengua poética de Góngora,* Madrid, 1935.

Anderson Imbert, Enrique, *Historia de la literatura hispanoamericana,* México, 1954.

Aub, Max, *La poesía española contemporánea,* México, 1954.

Ávila, Hermana Mary, C.S.J., "Principios cristianos en los cuentos de Rubén Darío," *Revista Iberoamericana,* XXIV (enero-junio, 1959), 29-39.

Banville, Théodore de, *Les cariatides,* Paris, 1877.

——, *Les exilés,* Paris, 1875.

——, *Les stalactites,* Paris, 1873.

——, *Petit traité de poésie française,* Paris, 1894.

Bartlett, John, *Familiar Quotations,* 13th ed., Boston, 1955.

Baudelaire, Charles, *Les fleurs du mal,* Montréal, 1943.

Bazin, Robert, *Historia de la literatura americana en lengua española,* trans. Josefina A. de Vázquez, Buenos Aires, 1958.

Bécquer, Gustavo Adolfo, *Las rimas y otras poesías,* Barcelona, 1949.

——, *Rimas,* Madrid, 1936.

Bellini, Giuseppe, *Dalle Origini al Modernismo,* Milano, 1959.

Bello, Andrés, *Colección de poesías originales,* Paris, 1870.

——, *Estudios gramaticales,* Caracas, 1951.

Belmas, Antonio Oliver, *Este otro Rubén Darío,* Barcelona, 1960.

Blanco Aguinaga, Carlos, *Unamuno, teórico del lenguaje,* México, 1954.

Blanco-Fombona, Rufino, *El modernismo y los poetas modernistas,* Madrid, 1929.

Borghini, Vittorio, *Rubén Darío e il modernismo,* Genova, 1955.

Brunetière, Ferdinand, *Essais sur la littérature contemporaine,* Paris, 1896.

Bucklin, L. B., "Some Spanish Words Derived from the Roman Liturgy," *Hispanic Review,* XXV (Jan., 1957), 50-62.

Calmettes, Fernand, *Leconte de Lisle et ses amis,* Paris, 1902.

Cansinos-Assens, R., *La nueva literatura,* Madrid, 1927.

Capdevila, Arturo, "Rubén Darío," *Nosotros,* XXI (1916), 288.

——, *Rubén Darío, "un bardo rei,"* Buenos Aires, 1946.

Cassou, Jean, *Panorama de la littérature espagnole contemporaine,* Paris, 1931.

Cestero, Tulio Manuel, *Rubén Darío, el hombre y el poeta,* Habana, 1916.

Coester, Alfred, *The Literary History of Spanish America,* New York, 1916.

Contreras, Francisco, *Rubén Darío. Su vida y su obra,* Barcelona, 1930.

Corominas, Juan, *Diccionario crítico etimológico de la lengua castellana,* 4 vols., Madrid, 1954-1957.

Darío, Rubén, *Azul . . .,* Buenos Aires, 1950.

——, *Cuentos completos,* ed. Ernesto Mejía Sánchez, México, 1950.

——, *Obras completas,* 22 vols., Madrid, [1917-1919?].

——, *Obras poéticas completas,* Madrid, 1941.

——, *Obras poéticas completas,* 6th ed., Madrid, 1949.

——, *Poesías,* ed. Ernesto Mejía Sánchez, México, 1952.

——, *Prosas profanas,* Paris, 1901.

Daudet, Alphonse, *Oeuvres complètes,* Paris, 1899.

Desonay, Fernand, "Le rêve hellénique chez les poètes parnassiens," *Bibliothèque de la Revue de Littérature Comparée,* L (1928), 1-420.

Díaz-Plaja, Guillermo, *La poesía lírica española,* Barcelona, 1948.

——, *Modernismo frente a noventa y ocho,* Madrid, 1951.

——, *Rubén Darío: la vida, la obra,* Barcelona, 1930.

Diccionario enciclopédico hispano-americano, 28 vols., Barcelona, 1887-1910.

Díez-Canedo, Enrique, *La nueva poesía,* México, 1942.

Donadíu y Puignan, Delfín, *Novísimo diccionario enciclopédico de la lengua castellana,* 4 vols., Barcelona, [1889-1899?].

Donoso, Armando, "La juventud de Rubén Darío," *Nosotros,* XXXI (abril, 1919), 443-528.

Doyle, Henry Grattan, *A Bibliography of Rubén Darío (1867-1916),* Cambridge, Mass., 1935.

Englekirk, John E., *Edgar Allan Poe in Hispanic Literature,* New York, 1934.

——, "El hispanoamericanismo y la generación del 98," *Revista Iberoamericana,* II (noviembre, 1940), 321-351.

Espinosa, Horacio, *Rubén Darío,* Managua, 1944.

Estève, Edmond, *Leconte de Lisle; l'homme et l'oeuvre,* Paris, [1923?].

Fath, R., *L'influence de la science sur la littérature française dans la seconde moitié du XIX⁰ siècle,* Lausanne, 1901.

Flaubert, Gustave, *La tentation de Saint Antoine,* Paris, 1924.

Floripe, Rodolfo, "Rubén Darío y Jules Lemaître: una fuente secundaria de *Azul,*" *Revista Iberoamericana,* XVII (enero, 1952), 285-292.

Fogelquist, Donald F., "El carácter hispánico del modernismo," *La cultura y la literatura iberoamericana,* México, 1957, VII, 139-146.

——, "The Literary Collaboration and the Personal Correspondence of Rubén Darío and Juan Ramón Jiménez," *University of Miami Hispanic-American Studies,* (Feb., 1956), pp. 1-47.

García Calderón, Ventura, *Semblanzas de América,* Madrid, 1920.

García-Girón, Edmundo, "El modernismo como evasión cultural," *La cultura y la literatura iberoamericana,* México, 1957, VII, 131-137.

——, "La adjetivación modernista en Rubén Darío," *Nueva Revista de Filología Hispánica,* XIII (1959), 345-351.

——, "La azul sonrisa. Disquisición sobre la adjetivación modernista," *Revista Iberoamericana,* XX (marzo, 1955), 95-116.

Gautier, Théophile, *Émaux et camées,* Paris, 1887.

——, *Histoire du Romantisme,* Paris, 1874.

——, *Les jeunes-France,* Paris, 1875.

——, *Poésies complètes,* ed. René Jasinski, 3 vols., Paris, 1932.

Gavaldá, Antonio C., *Pensamientos de Rubén Darío,* 2nd ed., Barcelona, 1957.

Gayley, Charles Mills, *The Classic Myths in English Literature and Art,* New York, 1939.

Goncourt, Edmond et Jules de, *L'amour au dix-huitième siècle,* Paris, 1875.

——, *L'art au dix-huitième siècle,* Paris, 1895.

——, *La femme au dix-huitième siècle,* 2 vols., Paris, [1923?].

González, Manuel Pedro, *Notas en torno al modernismo,* México, 1958.

González-Blanco, Andrés, *Los contemporáneos,* Paris, 1906.

G[onzález] Prada, Manuel, *Pájinas libres,* Paris, 1894.

Gordon, Alan M., *Verb Creation in the Works of José Martí: Method and Function,* unpub. Ph.D. thesis, Harvard, 1956, typewritten.

Guérin, Maurice de, *"Le centaure" et "La bacchante,"* ed. E. Decahors, Toulouse, 1932.

Guiraud, Pierre, *Index du vocabulaire du symbolisme,* 4 vols., Paris, 1953.

Gutiérrez Nájera, Manuel, *Poesías completas,* ed. Francisco González Guerrero, 2 vols., México, 1953.

Hamilton, Edith, *Mythology,* New York, 1959.

Henríquez Ureña, Max, *Breve historia del modernismo,* México, 1954.

——, *El retorno de los galeones,* Madrid, 1930.

——, "Las influencias francesas en la poesía hispanoamericana," *Revista Iberoamericana,* II (noviembre, 1940), 401-417.

——, *Rodó y Rubén Darío,* La Habana, 1918.

Henríquez Ureña, Pedro, *Ensayos críticos,* La Habana, 1905.

——, *La versificación irregular en la poesía castellana,* Madrid, 1933.

——, *Literary Currents in Spanish America*, Cambridge, Mass., 1945.

Henry, Albert, *Langage et poésie chez Paul Valéry*, Paris, 1925.

Heredia, José María de, *Les trophées*, Paris, [1898?].

——, *Poésies complètes*, Paris, 1924.

Hérold, A. Ferdinand, *Au hasard des chemins*, Paris, 1900.

Highet Gilbert, *The Classical Tradition*, New York, 1949.

Homer, *The Iliad*, trans. Richard Lattimore, Chicago, 1951.

Horace, *Odes*, ed. H. E. Butler, London, 1929.

Huarte Morton, Fernando, "El ideario lingüístico de Miguel de Unamuno," *Cuadernos de la Cátedra Miguel de Unamuno*, V, 1954, 5-183.

Hugo, Victor, *La légende des siècles*, ed. Jacques Truchet, Paris, 1950.

Jasinski, René, *Histoire de la littérature française*, 2 vols., Paris, 1947.

Lacau, María Hortensia and Mabel Manacorda de Rosetti, "Antecedentes del modernismo en la literatura argentina," *Cursos y Conferencias*, XXXI (abril-junio, 1947), 163-192.

Laín Entralgo, Pedro, *La generación del noventa y ocho*, Buenos Aires, 1947.

Lapesa, Rafael, *Historia de la lengua española*, 2nd ed., Madrid, 1950.

Laprade, Victor de, *Oeuvres poétiques*, 6 vols., Paris, [1878-1881?].

——, *Questions d'art et de morale*, Paris, 1861.

Leconte de Lisle, [Charles Marie René], *Poésies complètes*, Paris, 1858.

——, *Poèmes antiques*, Paris, [1886?].

——, *Poèmes barbares*, Paris, [1881?].

Lefèvre, André, *Les merveilles de l'architecture*, Paris, 1870.

LeFort, Emilio Carlos, "Rubén Darío and the 'Modernista' Movement," *University of Miami Hispanic-American Studies*, (Jan., 1941), pp. 220-237.

Leguizamón, Julio A., *Historia de la literatura hispanoamericana*, 2 vols., Buenos Aires, 1945.

Lida de Malkiel, María Rosa, *Juan de Mena*, México, 1950.

Liddell, Henry George and Robert Scott, *A Greek-English Lexicon*, 8th ed., Oxford, 1897.

Littré, Emile, *Dictionnaire de la langue française*, 4 vols., Paris, 1885.

Louys, Pierre, *Les poëmes de Pierre Louys*, ed. Yves-Gerard le Dantec, 2 vols., Paris, 1945.

Lugones, Leopoldo, *Rubén Darío*, San José, 1916.

Mallarmé, Stéphane, *Poésies*, Paris, 1949.

Mallo, Jerónimo, "Las relaciones personales y literarias entre Darío y Unamuno," *Revista Iberoamericana*, IX (febrero, 1945), 61-72.

Mapes, Erwin K., *Escritos inéditos de Rubén Darío*, New York, 1938.

——, *L'influence française dans l'oeuvre de Rubén Darío*, Paris, 1925.

Marasso, Arturo, *Rubén Darío y su creación poética,* ed. definitiva, Buenos Aires, 1954.

Martino, Pierre, *Parnasse et Symbolisme,* Paris, 1925.

Mejía Sánchez, Ernesto, "Las humanidades de Rubén Darío. Años de aprendizaje," *Libro jubilar de Alfonso Reyes,* México, 1956, pp. 243-263.

———, *Los primeros cuentos de Rubén Darío,* México, 1951.

Meléndez Valdés, Juan, *Odas anacreónticas y otros poemas,* Barcelona, 1944.

Ménard, René Joseph, *La mythologie dans l'art ancien et moderne,* Paris, 1878.

Mendès, Catulle, *Bacchus,* Paris, 1909.

———, *L'art d'aimer,* Paris, 1894.

———, *La légende du Parnasse contemporain,* Bruxelles, 1884,

———, *Les braises du cendrier. Nouvelles poésies,* Paris, 1900.

Menéndez y Pelayo, Marcelino, *Edición nacional de las obras completas,* 62 vols., Santander, 1949-1955.

Metzidakis, Philip, "Unamuno frente a la poesía de Rubén Darío," *Revista Iberoamericana,* XXV (julio-diciembre, 1960), 229-249.

Monguió, Luis, "Sobre la caracterización del modernismo," *Revista Iberoamericana,* VII (noviembre, 1943), 69-80.

Monner Sans, José María, *Julián del Casal y el modernismo hispanoamericano,* México, 1952.

Musset, Alfred de, *Poésies,* 2 vols., Paris, 1867.

Noël, Georges, "La poésie impersonelle et M. Leconte de Lisle," *Revue Contemporaine,* LXXV (1870), 662-681.

Normand, J. F., "Las ideas políticas de Rubén Darío," *Revista Iberoamericana,* II (noviembre, 1940), 435-440.

Oates, Whitney Jennings and Charles Theophilus Murphy, *Greek Literature in Translation,* New York, 1944.

Ortega y Gasset, José, *Vieja y nueva política,* Madrid, 1914.

Ovid, *Ars amatoria,* ed. J. H. Mozley, London, 1929.

———, *Metamorphoses,* ed. Frank Justus Miller, London 1916.

Oxford Classical Dictionary, Oxford, 1949.

Parish, Helen Rand, "El camino de la muerte, estudio psicológico del tema de la muerte en las poesías de Rubén Darío," *Revista Iberoamericana,* V (mayo, 1942), 71-86.

Peers, E. Allison, *A critical anthology of Spanish verse,* Berkeley, 1949.

Peyre, Henri, *L'influence des littératures antiques sur la littérature française moderne,* New Haven, 1941.

———, *Louis Ménard, 1822-1901,* New Haven, 1932.

Planche, Gustave, "La poésie en 1853," *Revue Des Deux Mondes,* III (1853), 1192-1215.

Plowert, Jacques, *Petit glossaire,* Paris, 1888.

Quintana, Manuel José, *Poesías,* Madrid, 1927.

Quintana González, Octavio, *Apreciaciones y anécdotas sobre Rubén Darío,* León, Nicaragua, 1950.

Real Academia Española, *Diccionario de la lengua castellana,* 6 vols., Madrid, 1726-1739.

——, *Diccionario de la lengua española,* 15th ed., Madrid, 1925.

——, *Diccionario de la lengua española,* 16th ed., Madrid, 1936.

——, *Diccionario de la lengua española,* 18th ed., Madrid, 1956.

Richepin, Jean, *Grandes amoureuses,* Paris, 1896.

Riley, H. T., ed., *Dictionary of Latin Quotations,* London, 1859.

Rimbaud, Arthur, *The Illuminations,* trans. Louise Varèse, New York, 1946.

Rodó, José Enrique, *Cinco ensayos,* Madrid, [1915?].

——, *Hombres de América,* Montevideo, 1939.

Rodríguez Demorizi, Emilio, *Rubén Darío y sus amigos dominicanos,* Bogotá, 1948.

Ruiz Morcuende, Federico, *Vocabulario de D. Leandro Fernández de Moratín,* 2 vols., Madrid, 1945.

Saavedra Molina, Julio, "Bibliografía de Rubén Darío," *Revista Chilena de Historia y Geografía,* (julio-diciembre, 1944), pp. 114-132.

——, "Bibliografía de Rubén Darío," *Revista Chilena de Historia y Geografía,* (enero-diciembre, 1945), pp. 177-219.

——, *Los hexámetros castellanos y en particular los de Rubén Darío,* [Santiago?], 1935.

Sainte-Beuve, Charles A., *Poésies complètes,* Paris, 1910.

Salinas, Pedro, *La poesía de Rubén Darío,* Buenos Aires, 1948.

Samain, Albert, *Au jardin de l'infante,* Paris 1914.

Sánchez, Juan Francisco, *De la métrica en Rubén Darío,* Ciudad Trujillo, 1955.

Sánchez, Luis Alberto, *Escritores representativos de América,* 2 vols., Madrid, 1957.

Saralegui, Manuel de, "Escarceos filológicos," *Boletín de la Real Academia Española,* XI (1924), 70-75.

Schade, George D., "La mitología clásica en la poesía modernista hispanoamericana," *La cultura y la literatura iberoamericana,* México, 1957, VII, 123-129.

——, *Mythology in the "modernista" Poetry of Spanish America,* unpub. Ph.D. thesis, Univ. of California (Berkeley), 1953, microfilm.

Schulman, Ivan A., "Génesis del azul modernista," *Revista Iberoamericana,* XXV (julio-diciembre, 1960), 251-271.

Sequeira, Diego Manuel, *Rubén Darío criollo*, Buenos Aires, 1945.

Silva, José Asunción, *Poesías*, Santiago de Chile, 1924.

Silva Castro, Raúl, *Rubén Darío y Chile*, Santiago de Chile, 1930.

Silvestre, Paul Armand, *Contes pantagruéliques et galantes*, Paris, 1884.

——, *Sapho*, Paris, 1881.

——, *La sculpture aux salons de 1896*, Paris, 1896.

Sobejano, Gonzalo, *El epíteto en la lírica española*, Madrid, 1956.

Soto Hall, Máximo, *Revelaciones íntimas de Rubén Darío*, Buenos Aires, 1925.

Souza, Raymond, "Eucharistic Symbols in the Poetry of Julio Herrera y Reissig," *Romance Notes*, I (1960), 97-100.

Sully Prudhomme (René François Armand Prudhomme), *Poésies (1865-1867)*, Paris, 1883.

——, *Poésies (1868-1878)*, Paris, 1884.

Tailhade, Laurent, *Poèmes élégiaques*, Paris, 1907.

Toro y Gisbert, Miguel de, *Los nuevos derroteros del idioma*, Paris, 1918.

Torre, Antonio M. de la, "Consideraciones sobre la actitud político-social de Rubén Darío," *Revista Iberoamericana*, XIX (septiembre, 1954), 261-272.

Torre, Francisco de la, *Poesías*, ed. Alonso Zamora Vicente, Madrid, 1944.

Torres, Edelberto, *La dramática vida de Rubén Darío*, Guatemala, 1952.

Torres-Rioseco, Arturo, *La gran literatura iberoamericana*, Buenos Aires, 1945.

——, *Rubén Darío, antología poética*, Berkeley, 1949.

——, *Rubén Darío, casticismo y americanismo*, Cambridge, Mass., 1931.

——, *Vida y poesía de Rubén Darío*, Buenos Aires, 1944.

Trend, J. B., "*Res metricae* de Rubén Darío," *Libro jubilar de Alfonso Reyes*, México, 1956, pp. 383-390.

——, *Rubén Darío*, Cambridge, Eng., 1952.

Ugarte, Manuel, *Escritores iberoamericanos de 1900*, Santiago de Chile, [1943?].

Uhrhan, Evelyn C., "Notes on the 'Seminario Archivo de Rubén Darío,'" *Kentucky Foreign Language Quarterly*, VIII (1961), 37-41.

Unamuno, Miguel de, *Ensayos*, 2 vols., Madrid, 1945.

Valera, Juan, *Obras completas*, 46 vols., Madrid, 1905-1917.

——, *Romances y poemas*, Madrid, 1885.

Vargas Vila, José María, *Rubén Darío*, Madrid, 1917.

Vergil, *The Twelve Books of the Aeneid*, New York, 1883.

Verlaine, Paul, *Fêtes galantes,* Manchester, 1942.

——, *Oeuvres poétiques complètes,* Paris, 1951.

Very, Francis, "Rubén Darío y la Biblia," *Revista Iberoamericana,* XVIII (1952), 141-155.

Virgil, *Bucolics,* ed. C. S. Jerram, Oxford, 1887.

——, *The Georgics,* N. Y., 1912.

Zéréga-Fombona, A., *Le symbolisme français et la poésie espagnole moderne,* Paris, 1919.

INDEX